Lyndon Baines Johnson

Dennis Eskow

FRANKLIN WATTS
An Impact Biography
New York ★ Chicago
London ★ Toronto ★ Sydney

Photographs copyright ©: UPI/Bettmann Newsphotos:
pp. 1, 6, 7 bottom, 9 bottom, 10 bottom, 14 bottom;
NARA/The Lyndon Baines Johnson Library: pp. 2, 3, 4
top, 4 bottom, 5 (both Austin Statesman), 8 top (Billy
Watson), 8 bottom (Art Kowert), 9 top, 10 top, 11, 12 top
(Robert Knudsen), 12 bottom, 13 bottom, 15 (all Y.R.
Okamoto), 13 top, 14 top, 16 (both Frank Wolfe).

Library of Congress Cataloging-in-Publication Data

Eskow, Dennis.
    Lyndon Baines Johnson / Dennis Eskow.
      p. cm. — (An Impact biography)
    Includes bibliographical references and index.
    Summary: Examines the life and political career of
Lyndon B. Johnson, and explains how his foreign
policy failures overrode the successes of his domestic
programs.
    ISBN 0-531-13019-3
    1. Johnson, Lyndon B. (Lyndon Baines), 1908-1973—
Juvenile literature. 2. Presidents—United States—
Biography—Juvenile literature. 3. United States—
Politics and government—1963-1969—Juvenile
literature. 4. United States—Foreign relations—
1963-1969—Juvenile literature. [1. Johnson, Lyndon
B. (Lyndon Baines), 1908-1973. 2. Presidents.]
I. Title.
E847.E8 - 1993
973.923′092—dc20
[B]   92-43687 CIP AC

Contents

Acknowledgments

I couldn't have put this book together without the exhaustive help of my wife and friend, Patricia Carlson Eskow, who spent hours in libraries and sifting through books, helping me to find research sources and checking the accuracy of my bibliography. Finally, I want to thank Carl C. Alexander, Beverly Alexander, Ken Jones, and Michael Joyce, four guiding spirits in my life and literally the overseers of my success.

DME, N.Y.
January 1992

To Herbert O. and Marguerite Carlson,
who raised one of the greatest women
who ever lived and who helped me
to be a writer

Preface

Before reading anything about Lyndon Baines Johnson, you have to ask yourself what history is. To Henry Ford, who learned little from history and who made and lost fortunes sometimes almost by accident, history was "more or less bunk." Thomas Carlyle, an eighteenth-century thinker, once called history "the biography of great men." But he also said history was a "distillation of rumor."

As one studies the life of LBJ, history is written, rewritten, and revised. LBJ told a lot of tall tales and so did those around him. And so did many who wrote about him, sometimes on purpose and sometimes without understanding that they were passing down to the next reader stories that were often embellished.

Although he lived the most significant moments of his life before a national audience, Lyndon Johnson somehow managed to leave history with a murky picture of his personality and his actions. The picture is beginning to come into focus as of this writing.

A lot of assistance is needed to help a writer sift through the countless stories for shreds of truth, and I must report that many people helped me in my quest for a clear picture of LBJ's life. To the staff of the LBJ library in Austin who fielded occasional phone calls from New York and helped

Lyndon

Baines

Johnson

get me started on the book, I owe a debt of gratitude. To the workers at the New York Public Library Research Branch and the Pelham Branch, I also say thanks.

I met Lyndon Johnson briefly and entirely by accident just once in my life, on a crisp, cool afternoon in Marietta, Georgia, in 1968. There, Johnson spoke at a ceremony for the rolling out of a new Air Force transport plane. Our meeting lasted just seconds. I was standing next to Congressman Mendel Rivers near the speakers' platform when a group of Secret Service agents pressed toward the stage with Johnson in their midst. He had a way of walking briskly, yet at the same time stopping at just about every step to shake hands with those within reach. I got just such a handshake and for less than a second our eyes met. President Johnson seemed to bend toward me at that moment and he seemed much larger than life.

In a moment he was gone. I have met two presidents (Gerald Ford and Jimmy Carter) since then and have interviewed one (Carter) at length. Each man was impressive in his own right. But LBJ, with whom I had the least contact, impressed me the most in one sense: Somehow, in a matter of seconds, he managed to make me feel that I was important to him. It was the eye-to-eye contact that conveyed the message, and I will never forget it.

Despite the fact that he had a way of engaging people, Johnson made many enemies in his political career, and his biographers have for the most part been very critical of his life and presidency. He seemed to many to be reckless with federal money. Many others who were alive during the Johnson presidency remember bitterly the escalation of the Vietnam War under his leadership.

10

But history has shown Lyndon Johnson to be far more complex than his contemporary critics were willing to admit. He was a consummate politician, a man who lived to make the political system work in his favor. But there was a statesmanlike aspect to Johnson as well. He devoted himself to the cause of civil rights and to the extension of basic human rights to all Americans.

So, while his biographers cannot forget the starkly political side of Lyndon Johnson, he will also be remembered for helping bring about a new era of equal justice under the law.

He must have been a good father, because his daughter Lynda Johnson Robb told me so. She remembers her father with a fondness and respect that are extraordinary. The interview she gave me was very helpful in balancing my own political feelings against a more objective historical record.

A
West Texas
Boyhood

A fierce wind blew from the north, carrying relentless sheets of rain across the central Texas Hill Country. It had been raining for days and the Pedernales River was spilling over its banks and threatening to take some houses with it. This was a tough land to live in, as it had been for generations. And tonight, three generations would huddle together against the storm.

Folks alive that night could still recall the days of the Civil War. And many of them had ridden with the Texas Rangers as swarms of new Americans swept across the West, pushing aside Native American nations and opening up territory where no human had lived before. They had stopped along the way, building farms, ranches, and towns.

But now their minds were on the weather. The wind had been howling all day, and toward evening thunder began to rumble and lightning stabbed the plains. Along the Pedernales, folks hunkered down indoors, lit kerosene lamps, and prayed that the river would stop rising. The weather was so bad that the family doctor would not be able to answer the call to come to the home of Samuel Ealy Johnson, Jr., that night. Samuel's wife, Rebekah, was struggling in labor, about to deliver her first baby. His father, Samuel Johnson, Sr., ran to fetch a midwife.[1]

Hardly anyone would have tried to reach the humble ranchhouse where Lyndon Baines Johnson, thirty-sixth president of the United States, was about to be born. Only close family members were there to witness the event.

Texans, it has sometimes been said, are very fond of legends. And so it is with a little bit of doubt that we recall some of the details of Lyndon's entrance into this world before daybreak the next morning, August 27, 1908. The account of the storm has been disputed by several historians, although there is no question that at the time the river was swollen over its banks because of a particularly rainy summer.

For most of America it was a year to remember —a presidential election year. Theodore Roosevelt had been president for seven years, and the presidency was now being hotly pursued by William Howard Taft and William Jennings Bryan.

That August was a month of excitement across the United States. The six-month New York to Paris Auto Race ended with the Americans winning. In Atlantic City two men were indicted for gambling and a shocked *New York Times* headline on August 22 seemed to gasp: "Women gamble as well as men."[2]

In San Francisco, a Mrs. Bessie Seaman—robbed a year earlier of $50,000 in jewels—had $6,000 worth of gems recovered at a pawn shop. An alert pawnshop owner had recognized the value of some jewels someone tried to sell him and had notified the police.[3]

African-American inventor Booker T. Washington was telling a gathering of Baltimore businessmen: "There is no hope for the Negro race or any other people except in the direction of constructive work." He called for an increase in jobs and education for all races.[4]

The actress Billie Burke toured the country in a four-act comedy called *Love Watches.* Isadora Duncan, the dancer who spoke out for women's rights, was also touring the country. And the patriotic songwriter (he was proud to have been "born on the Fourth of July") George M. Cohan had his play *The Yankee Prince* running in a theater in New York's Bowery district. At a Seattle Exposition, Native Americans and Siberian natives were placed in a live display. A seven-passenger Model H Franklin Auto with a 42-horsepower six-cylinder engine cost $3,750. The top was extra. Taxicabs in the big cities were drawn by horse. Fashionable women's coats sold for $15.

Much of this world was far from the Southwest, where Lyndon Johnson was born. The area near the Johnson ranch and nearby Johnson City was a backwater of Austin, the Texas capital. There were no paved streets, no electric outlets, few cars, and no major highways nearby. Supplies came into Johnson City by mule-drawn wagon.

Hill Country was a world unto itself. And Johnson was a child of the Texas Hill Country. His ancestors had lived in Texas since the 1840s and around that Hill Country since the 1850s. On his grandfather's side, they had come from Georgia and had pushed as far into the hill country as a white man dared, given the constant threats of Apache and Comanche Indian attacks.[5]

His grandparents could clearly recall the days of Indian raids, even on their own property along the Pedernales. On a night in July of 1869, long before Lyndon was born, a young couple living near the river had been killed by Comanches. A posse was sent out to look for the killers, and Sam Johnson, Lyndon's grandfather, was among the men in the party.

At home, his wife, Eliza Bunton Johnson, was doing her chores and caring for Lyndon's aunt Mary who was still in diapers at the time. As Eliza worked, she heard approaching hoofbeats. And as she looked off into a nearby woods, she could see what was certainly a platoon of Comanches approaching. Eliza scooped up baby Mary and made a mad dash for the root cellar.

There she huddled behind a closed door with the baby, whose mouth she muffled with a diaper. For what must have seemed to her like a breathless eternity the raiders explored the Johnson property, then mounted their horses and left. Eliza Bunton Johnson had survived![6]

If the house where Johnson was born was humble, it certainly wasn't out of place in the Hill Country. In one abandoned log cabin nearby, the following inscription was found written in chalk on a wall: "250 miles to the nearest post office. 100 miles to wood. 20 miles to water. 6 inches to hell. God bless our home."[7]

15

In such an atmosphere it is difficult to say whether the Johnson family was considered a pillar of the community or just a slightly above average family with some rather offbeat characters in it. Lyndon's father, Samuel Ealy Johnson, Jr., was sometimes seen as a man of great stature and sometimes as a social outcast, depending upon whether he was in or out of public office. Although he hadn't gone to college, he managed to become a schoolteacher at an early age and at twenty-seven was elected to the Texas legislature.[8]

His son Lyndon showed early signs of leadership qualities. By the age of nine, his brother Sam Houston Johnson reports, Lyndon was the second father in the Johnson household. "He was like the foreman, you might say—the boss—and he got me and my sisters Rebekah and Lucia and Josefa to do the work like slopping the pigs. . . ."[9]

How much we can count on Sam Houston Johnson's report is open to debate. His biography of his more successful brother (*My Brother Lyndon,* Cowles Book Company, 1970) caused a rift between the two that was never quite repaired, and Sam's memories of Lyndon may have been clouded by personal feelings and a desire to say something important in the biography.

Still, even if Sam's biography in some ways differed from the truth, it did state that Lyndon was a good-hearted brother who always looked after his younger siblings. For instance, Sam remembered a crisis that occurred on his first day in school: "Just before noon I was up at the blackboard, trying to scribble my name, when I had a sudden urge to relieve my bladder. Not knowing what to do, I just stood there squirming like a worm. . . ." The result was that Sam wet his trousers right in front of the whole class. The teacher had someone fetch Lyndon, who rushed to the room, cleaned up the mess with newspaper, and, without a harsh word, led Sam home to change and be comforted by their mother.[10]

Partly because Lyndon was so much older than brother Sam and partly because their father was away at the state legislature so much, LBJ seems to have grown up faster than the other Johnson children. Sam Houston Johnson noted that before LBJ was a teenager a competition of sorts developed between the father and his oldest son. They competed for young Sam's affection, and they may even have competed for Rebekah's. Although the legislature didn't meet year round every year, it did meet for four months every two years, and Sam Ealy's political involvements went beyond merely attending sessions. He was a legislator who conducted campaigns between sessions, drumming up support for various causes.

Competition between father and son does seem likely. Rebekah and her husband often argued over his tough ways and particularly over his drinking. LBJ also disapproved of his father's frequent drinking binges.

In addition to making life around the house difficult, someone who drank excessively was also considered a criminal in the 1920s. Under federal law no one was allowed to sell alcohol for drinking purposes anywhere in the United States. But many people disobeyed the law, and it was changed by constitutional amendment in 1933.

LBJ's father made no secret of his drinking, and Lyndon made no secret of his opposition to it. Once, when he was about twelve years old, Lyndon got a bunch of the Johnson City children to join him outside the saloon and call out the names of their fathers. "Come on home! Come on home!" the children chanted. The men thought it was a great joke, and Sam Ealy offered Lyndon 25 cents (enough in those days to go to a movie, buy candy, and pick up a rubber ball on the way home) to leave and take his friends with him. Lyndon wouldn't take the money; he wouldn't back down.[11]

Eventually, Sam Ealy reportedly gave in and left the saloon, angry with LBJ all the way home. Not that LBJ grew up to become a teetotaler. He was known to drink in his teenage years and never totally abstained from drinking.

The Johnsons moved often between town and countryside. Until Lyndon was fifteen, they generally lived on the farm where he had been born. But at times they would move into Johnson City, named for LBJ's family, for brief periods.

They lived in humble circumstances, and although some neighbors remembered the family as being poor, this was more a matter of appearances than of actual circumstances. Unlike some others in the neighborhood, the Johnsons ate three meals a day and never wanted for shoes.[12]

Still, many in the neighborhood considered the Johnsons poor, partly because the family went through frequent economic dry spells when they flirted with poverty. But they never stayed broke for long since Sam Ealy Johnson was a man with enough political contacts to get himself some kind of work.

During the bad spells, young Lyndon found that he could get considerable attention from townspeople. Lyndon was a born actor and he used his dramatic ability to gain the sympathy of local adults—especially the merchants. The youngster would walk into a store wearing a long face and heaving sighs until the store owners lavished some food, drink, or other spoils on him.

The house where he grew up, which now stands as part of a remodeled LBJ museum, had two bedrooms, a living room, and a dining room. There was a screened-in porch where the younger Johnson children slept. But Lyndon had his own room.[13]

Although the competition between LBJ and his dad appears to have begun early, there was no real resentment until Lyndon's teenage years. Until then, he and his dad had engaged in good-natured competition and behaved toward each other as best friends. The elder Johnson would often bring his boy with him to Austin and let him walk the halls of the state legislature. Young Lyndon would watch his dad grab people by the lapels, pull them really close to him, look them straight in the eyes, and talk them into voting his way.

The way Sam Ealy Johnson could make people do what he wanted them to do was impressive. It was a habit LBJ would pick up years later. He was, friends said, the image of his dad.

LBJ began to rebel in his high school years, partly because of his father's drinking. The rebellion may also have been encouraged by his parents' frequent bickering and his mother's unhappiness with her lot. Rebekah had given up an imagined life of upper-class finery and had abandoned her old literary circle of friends for a new world of dusty farmers. Lyndon undoubtedly heard his mother complain.

Rebekah Johnson thought of herself as a woman of class and style, and she did have some formal education. Samuel Ealy Johnson was different—a dreamer who often gave his time and energy to political causes, such as fighting the racist and reactionary Ku Klux Klan. His political pas-

19

sions were probably stronger than his commitment to his family. And, indeed, he did give politics more attention.

As LBJ became a teenager, his father's drinking became much more of an embarrassment and it served to emphasize how much more concern Sam showed his political position than he did his own family. In fact, Sam supposedly drank so much in those high school years of Lyndon's that he would stagger to his car and drive it to the gate of the Johnson ranch; here he would get one of Lyndon's friends to open the gate for him. Lyndon's friend Ben Crider recalled that Johnson would offer anyone around him a farewell drink right there in the car. But once he took off on one of his trips to the capitol in Austin he didn't drink.[14]

Devoted as he was to politics, Sam Ealy Johnson was never much of a rancher or farmer. He was unable to keep up the property on which the family lived, and he could not make any money from the land. His failures as a rancher and farmer were directly traceable to his absenteeism from home. Having Sam Ealy Johnson gone from the house to attend the legislative sessions in Austin apparently made a deep impression on Lyndon. He began to openly challenge his father's authority on the rare occasions when the older Johnson would come home.

Later, when Lyndon was a well-known politician, he said things that seemed almost calculated to punish his dead father. In describing a program to encourage farmers to live on the land, Johnson was to write: "We ranchers have a saying about absentee ownership: 'The footprints of the owner are the best fertilizer any land can have.'" Clearly, Lyndon could recall that Sam Ealy Johnson had rarely put a footprint on his family farm.[15]

It might have been the frequent absences of his father that caused Lyndon Johnson to seek older friends—and to get into now-legendary adventures. One of his best childhood friends, Ben Crider, was seven years older than Lyndon. "He wanted to run with older people," Crider remembered. "Usually about five to ten years older. He was a very brilliant young man, and the boys his age just wasn't [sic] in his class mentally."[16]

Even the school itself wasn't in his class. The schoolhouse was used by all grades up to the eleventh, which is where school ended for most kids in the county in 1924, the year Lyndon graduated from high school.

He had finished school in another county by staying with relatives and now returned to Johnson City. Lyndon's mother and father wanted him to go to college, but he was uninterested and so they told him to get a job.

In the summer of 1924 the state of Texas was building a highway between Austin and Johnson City. Boards had to be cut for the roadbed, and gravel had to be pounded in the hot summer sun. The work paid $2 a day, a fair wage at the time.

Lyndon got a job with the road gang, but it wasn't to last long. That summer he got into one of the worst situations of his young life. The story has been told by many people in many different ways—as have many stories about Lyndon—but the one point on which everyone seems to agree is that Lyndon was driving his father's car with a group of beer-drinking friends when he ran the car into a ditch. It was seriously damaged, and his friends recall taking up a collection, some say, to cover the repairs. But even that wasn't enough to calm down the hot-tempered Sam Ealy Johnson.[17]

Lyndon slept in the car the night of the accident and made his way south to stay with his cousins the Roper family in their home in Robstown on the Gulf Coast near Corpus Christi, about 200 miles south of Houston. At least he would avoid a humiliating beating from his father. And he might have escaped the road gang work, which he despised. It seems that Lyndon had thoughts of getting clerical work and might even have gotten it for a very short period, if we believe one of the interviews he gave later in life.[18]

Whatever the truth, he wound up working in a cotton gin, which may have been more physically demanding than the road gang. Before the summer of 1924 was over, the fifteen-year-old Lyndon wanted to go home. He didn't want to admit to his father that he couldn't handle the work, so he had Ben Crider get a message to Sam Ealy Johnson through someone else.[19]

Sam telephoned Lyndon and promised not to punish him for the wrecked car if he would come home. Lyndon did, but the summer of 1924 held yet one more great adventure.

A Life
of Adventure

Lyndon's teenage adventure would have been memorable for any young person. But to understand just how important it was to him, we have to look at the way his mother treated him as he was growing up.

Rebekah Baines Johnson thought of herself as quite an educated woman, and she gave Lyndon his thoughts of a great life far away from the Texas hill country. She had been born into a literate family. Her father, Joseph Wilson Baines, the editor and publisher of an influential newspaper, had taught her to read and to appreciate poetry and history. She read Browning and Tennyson and early Texas history.[1] So preoccupied was she with the proper education of the landowning class, that she even gave elocution lessons to the young girls who lived in the area.

The idea of an elocution lesson was to learn the "proper" pronunciation of English words and the "proper" selection of words in conversation. Those concerned with such things considered Texas accents and street language to be the mark of an inferior upbringing. Mrs. Johnson actually looked at elocution as part of a classical upbringing in which one read all the great books of the world and spoke well on important and intellectual things. Some of this rubbed off on Lyndon. For instance, she taught him to memorize poems before he was five.

Another account tells of Rebekah walking through the gate of the Johnson ranch after school, reading aloud from a book and coaxing Lyndon in his studies as he tagged behind her.[2]

Some people might have considered Lyndon a mama's boy. As an infant his mother had curled his shoulder-length hair and sometimes dressed him in clothes usually reserved for little girls. Even as he grew too old for that sort of thing, Lyndon continued to be dressed in short pants and cowboy suits by a mother who adored him.

Rebekah continued as Lyndon's mentor through high school, hounding him to study and dreaming of his future greatness. At one time he is supposed to have declared that he would one day become president of the United States, a statement that caused his young friends to laugh.

Getting through high school was a painful process for Lyndon. He sometimes did poorly and he sometimes did very well, depending upon how much he liked the subject. His favorite subjects were English and history; he found mathematics, particularly geometry, and science difficult. And he flunked gym class once, reportedly for cutting classes.

Rebekah Johnson had long moments of depression thinking that her son could grow up to be very much like his father. Lyndon had a foolish streak—displayed in his occasionally dangerous driving habits, fistfights, and pranks—that often caused his parents to argue over his future.

The car accident that sent him scurrying from home was actually the second that Lyndon had had with his father's cars. And he was a prankster. He and his friends would stay out until all hours of the morning. In one of their escapades very late one night, they sneaked up on the home of a local schoolteacher who was dating the local school superintendent. Lyndon and his friends piled boxes under her living-room window and took turns watching the two elders apparently do more than hold hands. A lot of different stories have been told about what Lyndon and his friends saw. No one can say which stories, if any, are true, but all the stories point to the same kind of mischief.[3]

Even with all of this, he managed to graduate from high school. Rebekah wasted little time in pushing him to go to Southwest Texas State Teachers College in San Marcos. Although the school lacked the great reputation that the state university in Austin had, it would be less expensive and Rebekah probably feared that her beloved Lyndon would simply get into trouble in the big city.[4] (Southwest Texas State University has an excellent reputation today, and its scenic hillside campus attracts many out-of-state students as well as Texans.)

Lyndon had other ideas, probably born of the

Lyndon

Baines

Johnson

poetry Rebekah had drummed into his head. Maybe his notions were aided and abetted by his wild friends. He wanted to run off and see the world. Walter Crider, Ben's brother, and Payne Roundtree, another older boy, were also anxious to leave the Hill Country. They wanted to go to California.

Lyndon, who turned sixteen that August, told friends that going to California would get him away from Rebekah, who had been giving him the silent treatment for weeks because he wouldn't decide to go to college. (LBJ has also told biographers that he ran off to California because "that's where I thought my fortune was." This is just another case of a lot of different things being said at the same time by Lyndon and about Lyndon.)

He and the four other boys involved each put $5 into a common fund and purchased a used Model T car. It was built of spare parts and didn't even have a roof. But it worked. His father tried to stop them from leaving, but Rebekah apparently gave at least quiet assent to the romantic trip. Lyndon would be taking flight in a way Rebekah could only have dreamed about. So Lyndon took off for California.[5]

It was a gamble, but not a completely insane one. Several other old Blanco County boys had moved out to California, and some reported that they were doing well. One of Lyndon's own cousins, Tom Martin, was practicing law there. He had set himself up in San Bernardino, and he was the first contact Lyndon made.

Even fifty years later, Otto Crider, one of the teenagers who traveled west with Lyndon and who stayed in California and made a real estate fortune, remembered it as "the most beautiful trip I ever made." The boys camped out along the way, building a roadside fire each night. By day they would take turns driving and lying on a mattress in the back seat, singing songs and having a good time.

There were no fast-food restaurants and no motels to stop at. The Texas boys worked at odd jobs in the fields and factories of California, and they found that life was both exciting and difficult. Sometimes, while working as grape pickers at very low wages, they lived on the grapes they picked.

Lyndon worked at such jobs for a few months, then went to work in his cousin Tom's Los Angeles law office. It was the perfect job for him; he ran errands and observed his cousin preparing to go to court.

Shortly after Lyndon went to work for his cousin, Tom called his father, lawyer Clarence Martin, to come from Texas and help out with a murder trial.

According to Sam Houston Johnson (LBJ's younger brother), Clarence Martin talked over the trip with Rebekah Johnson and agreed to bring Lyndon back to Texas when the trial was over. And, with some protests, Lyndon finally agreed to come home.[6]

Lyndon was finally ready to turn his back on the life of a drifter and settle down. As Rebekah wished, Lyndon now agreed to go to Southwest Texas State Teachers College in San Marcos. It was a small school with about 700 students, most of them the children of farmers and merchants from small towns.

There were a few Mexican-American students, but most were of European extraction. The small school placed serious rules of conduct on the students. They had to live in approved local board-

Lyndon

Baines

Johnson

ing houses. There was an 11 P.M. curfew, and that meant that no Teachers College student could be caught out of doors beyond that hour. Church attendance was required. Girls and boys could not ride together in cars. Girls' skirts had to cover their knees.

Johnson City High School was not fully accredited, so Lyndon had to take a six-week remedial course before his college career could begin. His first English paper was so good that his teacher thought Lyndon had been planted there as a joke. But he barely passed geometry, an exam for which he crammed with his mother the night before the test.[7]

With hard work he managed to complete the remedial course and made it into San Marcos to begin yet another adventure, one that would give him a taste for political campaigning and power. Actually, the groundwork had probably been firmly set in his boyhood. Lyndon was used to talking with the adults and ignoring the people his own age.

Now at San Marcos he could apply that to a new way of living: associating with those in power. As it was with many other San Marcos students, Lyndon had to work his way through college. And also as it was with many others, he took his first job with the campus cleanup crew, a position most people didn't want.

Johnson worked at it for a short time with the zeal he would later apply to climbing the political ladder—and the strategy worked. Within weeks, his reputation as a good cleanup crew worker got him the next position he wanted, also one in which few students were interested—assistant to the janitor in the science building. He used this job to catapult himself into the biggest plum of all: assistant to the secretary to the president of the college. It was classic LBJ.[8]

Although he quickly became close to the adults in power at school, he had more trouble with the circles of power among people his own age. Not that he didn't succeed a little. Through his connections with the college president, he managed to room with one of the most popular young men on campus; this gave him access to a lot of important social gatherings.

But Lyndon wasn't a big-time athlete, wasn't from a wealthy and powerful family, and didn't have any other weapons to work his way into the inner circle at San Marcos.

The inner circle called themselves the Black Stars, and to become part of their group you had to be a pretty important student. LBJ could not get admitted. But he noticed that the Black Stars, although considered the cream of the crop, represented only a small minority of the students. This sort of observation led to behavior that later would make him one of the most powerful members of the Democratic party.

Most people are not football heroes or cheerleaders. He began to realize that he could start his own inner circle by organizing the campus outcasts—in Sam Houston Johnson's words, "the skinny four-eyed president of the Biology Club and then the chubby editor of the yearbook." He told them they had brains and that brains were just as important as muscle. Maybe more important. Before too long LBJ had organized a group of campus outcasts who began to call themselves the White Stars. And there were far more of them than there were Black Stars.[9]

The White Stars were to become the political power on campus, launching Lyndon into control of the student newspaper and other associations. He soon called the shots on who sat on student councils. Lyndon was in charge. But his big ears, tall lanky looks, big mouth, and pushy attitude had made him a laughingstock on campus, and the students didn't stop laughing just because LBJ had power.

It was as organizer of the White Stars that Lyndon became the great political deal-maker. Who could have appreciated the future power this clumsy young man would one day wield as he pressed his friend Willard Deason to run for class president? Johnson helped him meet the campus outcasts and line up votes one by one.

"It soon became pretty clear that I couldn't win," Deason noted. "That I was at least fifteen to twenty votes behind. Most of us were ready to throw in the towel, but Lyndon said no. He said 'This is a challenge, and a challenge is an opportunity.'"[10]

In addition to the White Stars and the Black Stars there was a third special-interest group, the YMCA group, young people whose social life centered on the local YMCA. Dick Spinn, the popular senior who ran on the Black Star ticket and against Lyndon's friend Deason, was also a member of the YMCA group. Could Lyndon split the vote?

"By the next morning—we voted early—at ten o'clock the election was over, and I had won by eight votes," Deason recalled. "It's the kind of thing I guess Lyndon did later in the Senate when he was majority leader. Until the last vote was committed you couldn't get him to stop."[11]

Johnson's politicking had just begun. You don't beat the most popular people in college without having a fight on your hands. From the day

Deason won the election, the Black Stars campaigned against him, portraying him as a wimp who could not accomplish anything in office.

Perhaps their efforts to undermine Deason's position would have paid off when the next elections came up the following April. But Lyndon had a trick up his sleeve. At the last minute he substituted another White Star for Deason and rendered all the arguments pointless. The April election was an even bigger victory for the now growing White Star party.[12]

And the White Stars were quickly becoming the new power center on the San Marcos campus. To the dismay of the popular Black Stars, Lyndon even won a seat for himself in student government, a seat which he probably shouldn't have won considering how unpopular he was. But Lyndon was trying out some ideas he may have learned at Sam Ealy Johnson's feet: learn the parliamentary procedure of the group and use it to take over.

Few people have any appreciation for the power of parliamentary procedure, and Lyndon Baines Johnson counted on that in his election for student legislature. Due to a lack of interest in student elections, students voted with complete casualness. They never paid attention to things such as how to define a member of a particular class—as a junior, a senior, etc.[13]

Lyndon and his friends stacked the deck in their own favor by getting the position of election-meeting chair for one of their own White Stars. He would open and close nominations so quickly that the opposition Black Stars couldn't even nominate a candidate of their own. The White Stars apparently filled the room with "everyone who could possibly pass for a senior," according to Horace

Richards, the White Star who became meeting chairman.[14] Lyndon and the White Stars carried the day and won the elections.

During the course of his career at San Marcos, Lyndon rose to power beyond anything he might have imagined. He became editor in chief of the weekly *College Star* newspaper, a position that paid a small salary and gave Lyndon a big power base.

He wrote editorials covering a wide range of subjects pertinent to students and to the greater community as well. In a February 1928 editorial Lyndon wrote: "Behind all the constructive work is a vision, a dream, a plan. Without this the work would lack spirit, organization and power. It is the great compelling force that puts forth the first effort of the worker, that sustains him in discouragement and cheers him in consummation of the task. It starts the ball rolling and keeps it going in every-day practice. Vision is the soul of work."[15]

It wasn't controversial or soul-stirring, but it showed some of the patterns of good politics: the marriage of opinion-making and rulebook knowledge combined with the marriage of special-interest groups, especially those left out of the normal political process.

Despite the power, Lyndon could not overcome his inability to win acceptance with the in-crowd. And, perhaps saddest of all, to win the woman of his dreams. He had changed his luck in politics, but he didn't know how to change it in love.

The Courtship
of Lady Bird

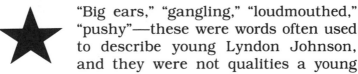"Big ears," "gangling," "loudmouthed," "pushy"—these were words often used to describe young Lyndon Johnson, and they were not qualities a young woman sought in a boyfriend. To make matters worse, Lyndon would often proclaim his intention of marrying a wealthy woman someday. Add to that his habit of clinging to people far older than he was and one gets a picture of a Lyndon Baines Johnson who did not do well when it came to matters of the heart.

Indeed, he often seemed star-crossed when it came to finding girlfriends, but not necessarily because he couldn't get a girl to pay attention. In fact, Lyndon often managed to land the most eligible girls around. He could be very charming, and young women also liked his outgoing and aggressive nature.

His first genuine fling at romance seems to have come around his senior year in high school. As with so many other Lyndon Johnson stories, this has many versions, but the consensus is that she was a natural choice for him. Her name was Kitty Clyde Ross, and friends said the two were in love.[1]

Kitty doesn't quite remember it that way. While acknowledging that she liked Lyndon and spent a lot of leisure time with him, she has said in an oral history: "Lyndon had several girlfriends. I went with him some. There was no such thing as going steady in those days; we didn't go steady, but we did go around together for a while."[2]

In his later years Lyndon apparently forgot the relationship, or he may have just pretended to forget it. Kitty recalls visiting LBJ and his wife, Lady Bird, in later years. Lyndon couldn't recall that he had ever kissed Kitty or even gone out with her. But it is typical of Johnson to dismiss an old acquaintance who might have slighted him in earlier times, and Kitty Ross is reported to have been one of Lyndon's most bitter disappointments in romance.

Kitty is described as having been pretty and intelligent, qualities Johnson had previously sought in older girls. Kitty Clyde was just one year older than Lyndon, and she thought he was very smart and had a promising future. The two of them represented one-third of the Johnson City High School graduating class, so it was inevitable that they would become close.

Kitty Clyde's family was thought to be the richest in the area. Her father, E. P. Ross, owned Ross' General Merchandising. Ross was an important figure and active member of the Methodist church, the leading church in the area. Few Johnson historians make much of this episode in Lyndon's life, but Robert Caro painstakingly researched it and gives it considerable attention in his widely acclaimed history of Johnson, and so it seems that the story is essentially true.

Kitty's father had married Mabel Chapman some twenty years before Lyndon and Kitty Clyde began to see each other. Mabel had gone out with none other than Sam Ealy Johnson, Lyndon's father, but Mabel's family did not like the Johnson family and her father forbade her to see Sam Ealy.

Twenty years later Lyndon was courting Kitty Clyde Ross and *her* father didn't like it. The qualities that had made her grandfather reject Sam Ealy were still evident in the Johnson family: Sam continued to be a heavy drinker, and the family couldn't pull itself out of economic distress for any length of time. Sam even lagged behind in his grocery bills, so that E. P. Ross and other merchants would send him a monthly bill with the word "Please!" scrawled across it.[3]

So frightened was the Ross family that Kitty Clyde would marry Lyndon that they personally pressed her into a relationship with her high school principal, a man thirty years old! And Ross saw to it that his daughter was seen around town with her new "boyfriend," always properly accompanied by her mother. It apparently irritated Lyndon a good deal, because one of his cousins wrote a parody, a song that has the same tune as a popular song but with different—and often funny—words.

As the Ross family sedan cruised through town with Kitty Clyde, the principal, and Mrs. Ross in it, Lyndon's cousin sang: "I don't like the kind of man/Does his lovin' in a Ford sedan;/ 'Cause you gotta see Mama every night/Or you can't see Baby at all."[4]

Even against the odds, Lyndon told relatives that he would ask Kitty Clyde for a date, and he did ask her to go with him to a local baseball game. Kitty Clyde said she would ask her parents. She soon returned and told Lyndon that she couldn't go with him. That was the end of his relationship with Kitty Clyde Ross.

But it was not the end of his pursuit of a rich woman. During his brief trip to California, Lyndon is supposed to have chased many women. But it was when he finally settled down at college in San Marcos that Lyndon began the earnest search for a woman with lots of money and potential.

Actually, he tried to start relationships with quite a few women, but in the end settled on one of the most sought-after young women in the area: Carol Davis.

How the affair with Carol Davis started and ended will always be covered in clouds of Texas storytelling. Some accounts say her father put an end to it quickly because of his politics. In his biography of his brother, Sam Houston Johnson says Miss Davis's dad had been sweet on their mother, Rebekah, before her marriage to Sam Ealy Johnson. Whatever the reason, the breakup left LBJ a very bitter college boy.

Carol was two years older than Lyndon and had graduated the year before Lyndon started at San Marcos. She was the richest girl in the area; she was also shy. Lyndon didn't even start going with her until he was about eighteen. In his later years, Johnson told biographer Doris Kearns that he fell in love with Carol Davis "the first moment we met."[5]

Others remember it happening a little less emotionally than that. In his biography, Robert Caro depicts Lyndon as courting Carol Davis with some care. He quotes one San Marcos student as saying that Lyndon bragged about Carol picking up restaurant checks and having money.

Was it bravado that made him perform for his friends and pretend that he only cared about her money? Or could he have painted an exaggerated romantic picture to impress biographer Kearns? Whatever the reason, the story remains essentially the same. His relationship with Carol Davis seems to have taken the same course as his relationship with Kitty Clyde Ross.

The lives of Lyndon Baines Johnson and Carol Davis were as different as if the two had grown up on different continents. To begin with, San Marcos residents lived in more prosperous and civilized conditions than those of Johnson City. The streets of San Marcos were paved, and the local grocery had grown into a wholesale and warehousing business so large that it provided groceries to general stores for miles around.

There were also more than 5,000 citizens in San Marcos, and one of the most prominent among them was a hardworking man who had served as mayor of the town when the streets had been paved and who also happened to own the huge grocery company. He was A. L. Davis, and his Baptist beliefs told him righteous men worked hard and lived clean.

Davis was as politically conservative as any of his neighbors, all of whom hated big government and big taxes. An essentially decent man, Davis refused to take part when the whole town attended a racist Ku Klux Klan rally.[6]

In later years LBJ and his brother, Sam, would tell so many different stories about this romance that writers eventually began to believe that A. L. Davis had kept his daughter Carol from marrying Lyndon because Davis was a KKK backer opposed to LBJ's father's brand of liberal politics. As with other such stories, there is only a tiny grain of truth in it.[7]

Davis apparently did know a good deal about Sam Ealy Johnson, but he loathed the elder Johnson's character, not his politics. He referred to the people of Texas Hill Country as "goat-herders" and considered them lazy. He had fled Hill Country as a young man to get away from its atmosphere of poverty and despair.

Davis raised four daughters in a beautiful home situated in town. Its porch was built so that on summer evenings he could sit on it and greet people as they strolled by. Inside was a tastefully decorated home filled with beautiful furnishings, more than one piano, and wardrobes filled with the fine things he had purchased for his daughters. A. L. Davis was certain that each of his girls would marry well. Especially Carol.

Carol was the favorite. She was industrious, obedient, and wise. She had graduated from San Marcos with honors. So it is not surprising that he viewed the appearance of Lyndon Johnson at his doorstep as a threat.

The boy looked like his father and walked with an arrogance that was unmistakable. Lyndon's favorite topic of discussion was himself. And his commitment to God was questionable at best. Lyndon did have higher aspirations than most of the "goatherds" from Hill Country, but there was a foolishness in his brashness.

The more Davis heard of Lyndon Johnson, the more sure he became that his daughter Carol could never marry this man. And the two youngsters were starting to get serious. She visited Johnson City twice and became acquainted with Lyndon's mother. On one visit to Johnson City, Carol and Lyndon went to a picnic with other young people and drew a lot of attention when they strolled off by themselves "hugging and kissing."[8]

Lyndon slowly began to push himself into the Davis household. He would often visit, and when he stepped up onto the Davis porch, Mr. Davis would grumble, then rise and leave. Things didn't get any better in the summer of 1928, when the Democratic party held its national convention in Houston. Lyndon managed to get press passes to the convention, and he asked Carol to go with him.

Carol, who was devoted to her father, was having second thoughts about the relationship. It was more than her father's pressure. She noted that she loved going to the movies, but that Lyndon hated it. She liked to play the piano and sing, but Lyndon was bored by it.

For Lyndon, politics was the only thing really interesting in life. He took Carol to the Democratic national convention, which she later described to friends as boring.

Later that summer, Carol Davis moved to Pearsall, where she took a room in a boarding-house and became a schoolteacher. She continued to exchange letters and telephone calls with Lyndon and saw him occasionally when he could get to Pearsall. But she met a postal clerk named Harold Smith who apparently liked all the things she liked and who met with her father's approval.

By the next year, with her father's blessing, she had become engaged to Harold Smith.[9]

For Johnson it was a crushing blow. He would remember Carol Davis with bitterness for the rest of his life. He was especially embittered by her father's rejection. In later years he would tell biographer Doris Kearns that it was he, and not Carol, who had ended the romance.

Even years later, when he was working in Washington, D.C., as a congressional assistant, Lyndon showed bitterness. On visits to his parents' home, if Carol Davis was in the area, Lyndon would avoid contact with her. He didn't see her face-to-face again until seven years after their breakup. At that time he was running for Congress. A. L. Davis was backing LBJ's opponent and had made a speech denouncing Johnson and his politics.

LBJ rose to speak in his own defense, but when he looked to the back of the auditorium he saw Carol Davis standing in the crowd. Johnson recalled that she looked pale and sad. Because of this he supposedly decided not to say anything against Davis.

Carol Davis was now out of the picture forever. And in 1934 the lovely Claudia Alta Taylor, after earning her second college degree, was given a trip to the East by her father. Her friend Gene Bohringer, who also knew LBJ, encouraged her to visit Johnson in Washington.

Claudia Taylor was a proper southern lady, so she neglected to call on LBJ during her trip. Despite her background and interest in journalism, she would not allow herself to so casually meet this young man.

Claudia was born on December 22, 1912, in

40 Karnack, Texas, an east Texas town. Her father

was a successful merchant/farmer, Thomas Jefferson Taylor, and her mother, Minnie Lee Taylor, was a wealthy southern belle who found Texas life difficult. Claudia's mother has been described as an emotionally troubled woman with frequent migraine headaches. She was also a reader of Greek and Roman mythology.

Claudia's mother was so vexed by the pressures of raising a family that she hired an African-American maid, Alice Tittle, to watch her younger children. It was Alice Tittle who gave Claudia, at age five, the nickname that stayed with her for life—Lady Bird, a title that described her small build and her tendency to hum tunes around the house.[10]

Minnie Lee died of a miscarriage when Lady Bird was only six years old. Lady Bird thus became the woman of the house long before her time. It may have contributed to her tendencies to be both shy and concerned about the operation of a household, tendencies that marked her later years in the White House.

Lady Bird's two brothers were sent away to boarding schools, but her father kept her with him as long as possible. For a brief time she would stay with him in the family store most of the day. Within months her father decided to send her to live with her unmarried aunt Effie in Alabama. Aunt Effie pushed Lady Bird's education in literature but had little interest in anything else.

After one year in Alabama, Effie and Lady Bird returned to Karnack and Effie moved into the Taylor home. There Lady Bird spent little time with other children because the local school was small and its students were often removed to go to work in the nearby farmers' fields. By the time she was in high school, she had become so shy that many of her fellow students expected her to remain single forever.[11]

After high school, Lady Bird went to a small Episcopal junior college for two years. She then decided to go to the University of Texas in Austin. The town was friendly and bustling and she blossomed there before heading east on the trip her father funded.

By the end of the summer of 1934, Lady Bird had returned to Texas, and while visiting Bohringer at his office at the Texas Railroad Commission in Austin, she finally met LBJ. (There are conflicting stories of where the two met for the first time. But this one appears in Johnson's own memoirs, so we'll stick with it.) He was, she was to recall later, the most outspoken, straightforward, determined young man she had ever met. "I knew I had met something remarkable, but I didn't quite know what," she was to say years later.[12]

Johnson had managed to do one thing: wangle a breakfast date with Claudia Taylor for the next morning. He might have been disappointed because she had decided to stand him up so she could make a business appointment for which she was running late. But she had to walk past where they were to meet, and he flagged her down. (Again there are different versions of this story.)

There she was, eating breakfast with the person she had expected to stand up and standing up her business appointment instead. Johnson went at Claudia Taylor the way a cowboy goes after a steer: relentlessly. In her own recollection in her biography, ". . . he just kept on asking me the most probing questions. What did you take in school? What's your family like? What do you want to do? He also was telling me all sorts of things I would never have asked him, certainly not on the first acquaintance."

They spent the whole day together, and by the end of that whirlwind date, LBJ had asked Claudia Taylor to marry him. She thought it was some sort of joke. She was just twenty-one years old, fresh out of college, and close to her father. She needed time to think. For the next four days, before he returned to Washington, LBJ hardly gave Claudia time to think. He saw her every day and made sure that she had little to think about but their possible future together.

LBJ was certainly not one to waste time. It was with great zeal and super speed that he courted Claudia Taylor, now known to history as Lady Bird Johnson. When they were apart, Lyndon wrote daily letters to her, letters filled with his dreams and plans. These were designed to sweep Claudia off her feet. And "designed" is probably a good word. After finishing a letter, LBJ is supposed to have asked fellow-congressional-staffer Gene Latimer to listen to a sentence and help with the punctuation or check the spelling of a word.[13]

The young man who proposed to Lady Bird on the first date apparently struck Claudia Taylor's father as husband material during their first meeting. Thomas Taylor, a local merchant and political leader of fair importance, was himself swaggering and sometimes arrogant. He seemed to be taken with Lyndon immediately and is reported to have told Lady Bird that night: "You've been bringing home a lot of boys up till now. This time you've brought home a man."[14]

LBJ made it a whirlwind courtship. He wasted no time in bringing Lady Bird home to meet his family. He drove her to the fabulous King Ranch to meet Congressman Richard Kleberg, his boss, and several other powerful Texans.

Lady Bird was a good name for this young woman who was as energetic as a Texas bobwhite and as delicate as a nightingale. Even years later, after living in Washington within the inner circle of national power, she was often seen walking briskly down the halls of the White House whistling or humming tunes from the latest Broadway shows like a cheerful and industrious bird.

The man she was to marry was not from a great family, but it was an old and important Hill Country family, and Lady Bird's father approved of Johnson's roots and encouraged her to marry him. LBJ was an industrious young man with a future, and that's what Lady Bird sought in a husband.

Oddly, as a couple they resembled Lyndon's own father and mother of a generation earlier. Sam Houston Johnson noted: "[Lyndon] himself hardly read a novel or poetry. . . . Lyndon admired Lady Bird's capacity to enjoy writers like Fitzgerald, Hemingway . . . and some Russian authors he had never even heard of."[15]

Lyndon had chosen a woman much more cultured and refined than he was. In the autumn of 1934, Lyndon Baines Johnson went to Texas with marriage on his mind. He again proposed to Claudia Taylor, secured her father's permission, and contacted his San Antonio friend Dan Quill to arrange the wedding. It was a Saturday morning when the phone rang at the Quill household. The call was from Karnack, Texas, about 350 miles away.

Lyndon told Quill that Lady Bird had accepted his proposal and that they wanted to be married that very night at an Episcopal church. "We haven't done anything," Lyndon told Quill. "And I wish you'd make the arrangements and we'll see you about six o'clock at the Plaza Hotel."[16]

Quill phoned his and Lyndon's friend Henry Hirschberg, a lawyer, and announced that Hirschberg would be the best man. Hirschberg had to break an engagement to get to St. Mark's Church in time to be the best man. And to meet the bride for the first time.

On November 17, 1934, with no family members present and no announcements, Lyndon Baines Johnson and Claudia Alta Taylor were wed. It was not the kind of wedding most girls dreamed of in those days. In fact, it was so rushed that Claudia Taylor was still discussing whether to go through with it when she and LBJ reached the door of the church.

Shortly before the ceremony began, LBJ decided it would be Quill and not Hirschberg who would serve as best man. And Lady Bird asked whether Lyndon had gotten a wedding ring. He had forgotten, so Quill reportedly rushed out of the church to a nearby Sears store and returned with a tray full of rings. The one the Johnsons chose cost $2.50, and it was Quill's wedding present to them.[17]

Lyndon married the kind of woman he had been seeking throughout his youth. Her father was a fairly prosperous businessman who had moved to Texas from his poor Alabama farm. At first Thomas Jefferson Taylor ran only the local general store in Karnack but later acquired cotton gins, small farms, and other properties.

His daughter Claudia was shy and intelligent. She had majored in journalism in college and was considered a promising student.[18]

She would be an asset to LBJ as a politician. Indeed, Lady Bird Johnson stood behind her husband and helped make him a success from the first day of their marriage. Now LBJ could take off politically. He had a trusted mate who could handle life in Washington as well as standing up as a model Texas wife.

But before we can launch into LBJ's political career, we should stop and see how he got to Washington in the first place.

Right Place, Right Time

 With the depression gripping South Texas in 1930, Lyndon began to panic about finding work to support himself at San Marcos. Businesses were closing all over Texas and the rest of the country, and no money was available for patronage jobs, the positions politicians give away. By using letters of recommendation from his college president and faculty members, the aggressive LBJ found a position in a poor school for Mexican-American students in Pearsall, a town even smaller and more impoverished than Johnson City. LBJ taught there for a brief period until a position for a speech teacher opened at Sam Houston High in Houston. LBJ's sister Rebekah took over his duties in Pearsall so that he could travel to Houston.[1]

In Houston he became extremely popular as a teacher and coach of the debating team. Students tried to reschedule other classes to get into Mr. Johnson's class. He was young and smart and he wanted to win. They wanted to win, too. It seemed he had found a home in Houston after just one year.

It was around this time that LBJ attended a political barbecue in Henly, Texas. Making the trip with his father, Lyndon was going to show support for Pat Neff, the former Texas governor who had given Sam Ealy Johnson a job when he had fallen on hard times. Neff was running for the Texas State Railroad Commission, and when it was his time to take the stage he didn't appear.

The master of ceremonies wanted to know if anyone present could speak for Pat Neff. Years earlier, LBJ's father might have been the man to do it. But the once proud Sam Ealy Johnson was stoop-shouldered and tired now and was in no condition to speak for Neff. LBJ stepped in and did the talking on Pat Neff's behalf—his first political speech. Not only was he making an unprepared speech but it was late at night and Lyndon was in the unenviable role of last speaker. Although he spoke briefly, the crowd appreciated his courage.

Welly K. Hopkins, a young candidate for Texas state senator who was present when Johnson stepped in for Neff, was impressed with LBJ's speech. He was even more impressed when he asked Johnson why he had done this for Neff and Johnson explained that Neff had helped his father during rough times. Lyndon felt he owed it to Neff.

LBJ went to work in the Hopkins campaign

using his newly organized San Marcos White Stars (the group of campus political outcasts he had organized) to campaign for Hopkins. Hopkins won by a landslide, and Lyndon Baines Johnson's political career was under way. Hopkins soon introduced LBJ to other politicians and LBJ's reputation began to spread.[2]

So impressed had Welly Hopkins been with LBJ's abilities that he called on him to help run the congressional campaign of Richard Kleberg, whose father was the most powerful rancher in Texas and owner of the breathtaking and famous King Ranch. LBJ accepted and even pressed some of his old White Star friends into service.

It was 1931 and LBJ was twenty-three years old. The young man who had vowed to become president of the United States was now looking opportunity in the face. It was a rugged election campaign in which Kleberg's opposition tried to paint him as a rich and powerful man with no love for the little people. Meanwhile, LBJ and Welly Hopkins made campaign speeches for Kleberg all over Texas. On November 24 the election was so close that it could have gone either way, but Kleberg won. LBJ asked Hopkins to press the new congressman for a job for LBJ in Washington.[3]

With the election over, LBJ returned to Houston and resumed his role as star teacher. His popularity was greater than ever. His students looked forward to winning trophies with him as their debating coach; indeed, some admired him so much that he would eventually put them to work politically.

But a few days after the election a phone call came from Congressman Kleberg. He needed a secretary. (In those days such jobs were handled mostly by men, who really acted as administrative

49

assistants, running errands, answering phones, and making appointments for the congressman. Typists were used to do the job we now associate with secretarial work.) Welly Hopkins had recommended LBJ for the job. Less than one week later, LBJ was on his way to Washington, D.C., and his new life.[4]

By the time he left for Washington, LBJ's personality was forged forever. He was a man with many faces. He could be extremely vulgar, hot-tempered, and pushy, as he had learned to be on the dusty streets of Johnson City and at San Marcos. And he could be poetic and giving as he had been in Pearsall and Houston. As one acquaintance would describe him later: "I think Johnson . . . was an actor on a big stage."[5]

But an actor needs tools. He needs experience and understanding, education and wisdom, and a certain inventory of credentials that make him believable. Lyndon Johnson, who had charmed his way through college, in 1934 enrolled in Georgetown law school as a night student. He reportedly studied law diligently and impressed his teachers as a man who was going places.

He was now a married man who *was* going places and who was building strategic alliances. Johnson impressed all of his colleagues with his incredible energy. Although he was saddled with a Texas regional accent and had trouble pronouncing certain words, he did well in casual, friendly political debates largely because of his knowledge of history.

"Lyndon dropped in my office almost every day," said Wright Patman, a congressman when LBJ arrived in Washington and later one of the most powerful men on Capitol Hill. "He wanted to talk politics. . . ." Sam Rayburn, for whom the main House of Representatives office building is named today, was chairman of the House Commerce Committee at the time and treated the young man like family. Rayburn had known Lyndon's father in the Texas state legislature and was practically a father to Lyndon.[6]

LBJ quickly set to work in Kleberg's office as a staff aide, dictating letters in answer to constituents' questions and following Kleberg all over the Capitol. He was industrious and also never missed a chance to enhance his own image and make his own connections.

Johnson's aggressiveness once embarrassed a fellow Texan, Robert Jackson of Corpus Christi, who sat with House members in the chamber on the first day of the session in 1931. It was quiet in the room, so he couldn't help but notice the lanky, clumsy-looking LBJ—"this tall countrified boy, talking loud and embarrassing me"—as LBJ pushed his way into a good seat. Johnson could not be ignored as he thrust out his big hand to anyone who would receive it and said, "My name is Lyndon Johnson. I'm secretary to Congressman Richard Kleberg of the 14th District of Texas." Jackson turned away from Johnson and tried to ignore him, but LBJ leaned toward him and tapped him on the shoulder; in a few minutes Jackson found himself greeting LBJ.[7]

As with many others who would follow, Jackson found himself helping the very man who had embarrassed him and made him feel uncomfortable. Jackson helped Lyndon get a room at the Dodge Hotel, a run-down residential hotel near the Capitol. The two even shared a bathroom. Jackson said they became "about as close as two people could be."

As he became familiar with the congressional **51**

Lyndon

Baines

Johnson

surroundings, LBJ was to flex the political muscle he had begun to build back in San Marcos when he ran errands for the college president. Just as that had led to important positions on campus and his eventual appointment as a teacher, his congressional errand-running seemed to be a key to political power.

As secretary to a Congressman, Johnson was eligible to join the "Little Congress," an inner circle of congressional aides. As with so many other organizations, the meetings of the Little Congress had come to be attended by just a few members, just barely enough to keep it going. And the group wasn't doing much more than talking and drinking coffee. But it was to provide Johnson with as much opportunity for taking over as had the students he rounded up for the White Stars.

At his very first meeting LBJ announced that he would run the following week for the open position of "speaker." (In organizations like the Little Congress, it is always difficult to get people to take leadership positions.) But here was Lyndon Johnson running for a position right after joining. He enlisted his new friend Jackson as a campaign manager. The following week a crowd of people eligible to join the Little Congress showed up for the meeting and asked to join. It was no accident that so many eligibles joined then. LBJ had herded them to the meeting the way a cattle driver herds steers. LBJ won the election by a 2-to-1 margin.[8]

As he had with the errand-running at San Marcos, Johnson used his post in the Little Congress to get close to the secretaries of some of the nation's most powerful legislators. Through this quietly powerful position he learned the names of friends and enemies back home; he also learned a lot of very personal things about members of Con-

52

gress. Johnson soon took a pay cut, resigned as Kleberg's secretary, and became a Capitol page (a page runs errands for members of the House). Johnson worked as a page while working for Kleberg in the evenings at no charge. By late 1933 LBJ was one of the best-known young men in legislative circles. No job was too unimportant or too dirty. In fact, LBJ showed very little ethical sense as he ran in the corridors of power.

In 1934, LBJ, his former Houston debate student Gene Latimer, and Kleberg's assistant secretary Luther Jones returned to Texas to help campaign for Kleberg's friend and fellow-Democrat Maury Maverick in his race for Congress. Jones remembers Johnson and Latimer working to distribute money to leading Mexican-American families. The amount reportedly depended upon the number of voters in the family. In other words, Johnson was buying votes.[9]

It apparently disturbed Jones, but Latimer and Johnson don't seem to have been disturbed by this type of corruption. (In fairness to Johnson, cheating of this type was widespread in Texas, and it has been widespread in American history. The Cook County, Illinois, Democratic party organization would years later scandalize the nation with vote-buying, and even double-voting by people who used the voter-registration cards of the dead.)

LBJ returned to Washington and redoubled his efforts to network with powerful men. In the summer of 1935 it finally paid off. LBJ was about to take a step that would launch him into a position of relative power within the growing federal government framework. President Franklin Roosevelt, trying to combat a badly depressed economy, organized the National Youth Administration, an

53

agency designed to create jobs for unemployed young people.

Roosevelt signed the NYA into being on a Tuesday morning. Before the sun set that day, LBJ had called powerful Texas Democrats Sam Rayburn, Alvin Wirtz, Maury Maverick, and Tom Connolly and proposed himself as the man to run the Texas office of the new agency. Having built a power base with some very old politicians, LBJ could now build one with the Texas voters. He could provide jobs for thousands of Texans of his own generation. And he could trade favors.

As he had with the errand-running at San Marcos, Lyndon took an undefined job and turned it into a powerful one. He worked tirelessly and got Texas millionaires to contribute supplies, money, and projects to get hundreds of young people working almost overnight.

LBJ accomplished so much in a few short months that he came to the attention of the NYA leadership in Washington. And when President Roosevelt's wife, Eleanor, visited Texas in 1936, she brought a group of reporters along as she visited NYA state headquarters in Austin.[10]

It was an opportunity for LBJ to intimate to friends and colleagues that his political career was becoming entwined with the popular and powerful Roosevelt White House. In fact, his support of Roosevelt launched LBJ into his congressional career. LBJ ran his first congressional campaign on a controversial national pro-Roosevelt issue which detractors labeled as "Supreme Court–packing."

Actually, President Roosevelt was merely exercising the powers of his office by trying to appoint judges to the High Court who seemed to agree with his programs. President Roosevelt felt that it was the most effective way to bend the balance of power in the federal government.

Constitutionally and historically, that balance had divided the federal government into three segments: legislative (Congress), executive (the president), and judicial. The president set the tone for the operation of the federal government. Congress inserted the voice of the people by having the last word over budgets. And the judiciary kept the entire operation in balance by hearing cases of new laws or the executive department's handling of old laws.

That was the ideal world. In the real world, each sector of government fought for as much power as it could get. And Roosevelt was doing what all presidents try to do—garnering the United States Supreme Court's power by filling vacancies created by the death or retirement of justices with his own appointees. In other words, he was stacking the Court.

Supreme Court–packing was so emotional an issue that a Philadelphia Methodist meeting, in a 104-to-25 vote, accused the Roosevelt plan of trying to "seize control of the safeguards of American government." It was no different in Texas. A dispatch to the *New York Times* on Sunday, March 7, 1937, said the 50,000 voters "in the [Texas] Tenth Congressional District may be the first to express themselves by ballot on President Roosevelt's proposal to reorganize the supreme court."

Polk Shelton, former district attorney of Travis County, Texas, announced that he would seek the office of congressional representative on a platform of "no yes-man judges," or no Court-packing. Lyndon Johnson, who resigned as state director for the National Youth Administration to run for the seat, stood squarely behind the Roose-

Right Place,

Right Time

55

velt proposal. The following month, on April 11, 1937, LBJ celebrated his election victory with reporters in Austin, the Texas capital. The Associated Press said Johnson, who had just had his appendix removed, "shouted his advocacy of President Roosevelt's court organization."[11]

Johnson said he considered his election "a vote of confidence" in Roosevelt's Court policy. Just beneath the surface of the pro-Roosevelt campaign, however, was the real Lyndon Johnson —the boy who had bullied his brother and sister into doing chores, the young man who brashly curried favor with his college's president to reach a point of power, the young man who vowed to marry a rich woman. In a brief period as Texas NYA director, LBJ had been showing Texas what it would get if it sent him to Congress. His campaign slogan was "He gets things done."

Indeed, as director of the Texas NYA he had gotten a remarkably large number of things done. And he did it in front of the public. He arranged a press conference upon his arrival in Texas as NYA chief. He told reporters at the Austin airport that he considered it his job to put himself out of a job. In other words, Lyndon Baines Johnson was stating that the end of the depression in Texas would be brought about by him, personally.

He then went on a whirlwind tour of Texas cities, explaining to the mayors of each—and to reporters who met him at each airport—how the NYA would operate. LBJ had learned a great deal from his congressional mentors, and now he was applying it. Get publicity. Get seen—and get seen with the right people.

Surrounding himself with loyal former students from Houston and with some of his old White Star allies, LBJ then started on the Texas economy. Johnson quickly set to work trying to reach the largest number of people. Through school aid, the NYA gave support to 18,000 college and vocational students.

He put young Texans to work building roadside picnic areas, restoring old public buildings, and even building ambitious recreation facilities with swimming pools and baseball fields. He also set up special programs for young women seeking to become nurses or homemakers. In a very short time, Lyndon Johnson managed to be at the forefront in restoring the confidence of young people in the future of Texas as well as America.[12]

After he was elected to Congress, LBJ simply reproduced what had made him successful with the NYA. He got things done. Johnson quickly became a popular Roosevelt man, popular both with other politicians and with Roosevelt himself. He was in the right place at the right time. This was an era in which bureaucracy was of major importance, and if Lyndon Johnson was good at anything it was bureaucracy.

Not long after his election he met President Franklin D. Roosevelt for the first time. The president had been fishing off the Texas coast in the Gulf of Mexico and wanted Johnson to greet him in Galveston. Johnson obliged with relish. This was an opportunity greater than errand-running at San Marcos, and LBJ was going to make the most of it.

He reportedly spent a good deal of time talking to Roosevelt about the Navy, a subject which previously had interested him little, if at all. But it was an important issue for Roosevelt, who during that first meeting is reported to have given LBJ a slip of paper with the name and direct telephone number of White House aide Thomas Corcoran, a political "fixer" who would use his influence to get Johnson a seat on the House Committee on Naval Affairs.

But Johnson wanted more than that seat. He wanted the president's influence. And for the next months and years he gained it and played it like a musical instrument. He pushed for federal construction projects in his own district, once again getting things done.

While many congressional representatives of his day centered their jobs around legislation that was being enacted in Washington, Johnson took care of his home district, getting federal funds for numerous projects that brought electric power, better highways, improved schools, libraries, and other advances to his district.

Nobody could appreciate that fact more than Herman Brown, the brains behind Texas's already powerful Brown & Root construction company and a man who understood the value of political power. From the year Johnson entered Congress he and Brown were political friends, LBJ helping Brown & Root get lucrative federal construction contracts, and Brown investing in LBJ's campaigns. Better still, Brown forced subcontractors who worked for him to give financial support to Johnson. It made an impression on Texans, who would see Johnson as part of the powerful and wealthy machine that ran the state.[13]

5

The Senate Deal-Maker

For Lyndon Johnson, a political machine existed to launch him into increasingly important positions. He had learned to work that machine in relatively short order, and it had brought him a seat in Congress.

But it was the real political brass ring, the highest height, that LBJ was reaching for—a seat in the United States Senate. That brought national recognition, that had clout. He took his first shot at a Senate seat in 1941. But the race was tough, and Johnson faced several opponents with greater visibility among Texans. He was defeated by W. Lee

"Pappy" O'Daniel, a flour merchant who once sang with a country band on WMOL radio in Fort Worth. Bags of his flour carried this corny verse:

> Hillbilly music in the air
> Hillbilly flour everywhere
> It tickles your feet—it tickles your tongue
> Wherever you go, its praises are sung[1]
> Pappy O'Daniel also happened to be governor of Texas.

How could a corny, homespun flour merchant defeat this man with all the connections back in Washington? Although the 1941 Senate race is the only election LBJ ever lost, it may be the key to his entire political life story. He was a man who worked hard to understand the rules of the organizations and government agencies in which he worked. He was a man who used these rules to gain power. But all his power couldn't help him if he didn't have the support of the people empowered to vote him in and out of office.

He had shaken hands with thousands of people and he had made powerful connections, but LBJ had few real friends, and people back home didn't know him. He was a Roosevelt man, not a Texas man. And Texas was in a much more conservative mood in 1941 than it had been when Johnson won his House seat. Where his initial Roosevelt connection had helped him the first time, his now stronger ties to the president seemed to hurt him.

It was President Roosevelt, in fact, who convinced Johnson to run. "Roosevelt wanted him to do it because he knew Johnson as a man he could count on for support," said Thomas G. Corcoran, a Roosevelt adviser and lawyer.[2]

Johnson lost to O'Daniel by less than 2,000 votes, and there were some in the LBJ camp who wanted a recount. There were also hints of voter fraud. But Johnson didn't ask for a recount, probably because he himself had purchased votes during the campaign. With money from Herman Brown, the Brown & Root construction company millionare who had amassed a fortune on projects Congressman Johnson had helped him get, LBJ had a virtually limitless treasure chest of support.

Johnson never expected to lose the election. And LBJ biographer Robert A. Caro believes that Johnson should have won, that O'Daniel's political allies stole the election—literally. Political pollsters in those days didn't have the kinds of staffs and tools at their disposal that they do today, and Johnson's pollsters figured on an impressive victory for their man. On Election Day, Johnson broke with Texas tradition and told the political bosses who backed him that they could report the vote count in their districts early. In Texas, that was a mistake if the election was close. After all, if the opposition knew how many votes you had, could they not simply fix the vote to give themselves just a few more? That seems to be what the O'Daniel camp did.[3]

As he had in his first congressional campaign, Johnson seized on a Roosevelt theme for his first Senate race. Roosevelt in 1941 was trying to convince Americans that the country was not going to be forced into the growing world war. "Your boys," he vowed, "are not going to be sent into any foreign wars."[4]

In his first campaign speech, LBJ promised: "If the day ever comes when my vote must be cast to send your boy to the trenches—that day Lyndon Johnson will leave his Senate seat to go with him."

It was typical LBJ rhetoric and was met with suspicion from several editorial writers. His detractors painted him as a loudmouthed coward.[5]

And there is little reason to believe that even LBJ believed what he was saying when he promised to go into the trenches of war.

He had joined the Navy as a reserve officer in 1939 and was a lieutenant commander (LTC) by the time he made his statement. But when America finally entered World War II about six months after LBJ's campaign speech, he managed to get himself desk jobs far from any fighting. He used his influence with President Roosevelt to get jobs inspecting naval installations and later negotiated a desk job in Washington. While some writers question his courage, one might also conclude that Johnson didn't want to be far from the halls of power. If going to combat would have won him a high position, it may be that LBJ would have jumped at the chance.

After the Japanese bombed Pearl Harbor, Hawaii, killing thousands of American sailors and sinking most of the U.S. Pacific Fleet, America plunged headlong into a war that seemed to be in the hands of the Japanese. During those weeks and months, LBJ toured the western states to inspect naval installations.

LBJ did finally get overseas. In April of 1942, Roosevelt ordered him to join a military inspection team heading for the South Pacific. They were to report to the president on how the war effort was going. His first stop was Melbourne, Australia, where he met with General Douglas MacArthur, the brilliant leader of America's Pacific effort. There followed days of hopping around the islands near Australia and at different military bases in that continent and country. And one morning, LBJ was invited to go along on a bombing mission. He didn't have to go but said he wanted to.

Johnson, at 6 feet 3 inches tall (192 cm), could barely squeeze into the space behind the cockpit of the B-26 bomber to which he was assigned. While the plane was going through preflight checkout LBJ had to urinate, so he stepped out of the aircraft. When he climbed back in, another officer was sitting in his seat and Johnson backed away and found another B-26 to ride in. Soon they were taking off on their mission. But as they came close to the target, one of the plane's engines died and they had to turn back.

The next minutes must have been the most memorable in LBJ's life. As the plane turned around, it was attacked by three Japanese fighter planes, Zeros, so named because they bore the Japanese national emblem, a picture of a rising sun that looks like a zero. LBJ's plane was hit with machine-gun fire. The Japanese fighters seemed to be playing with the bomber like cats with a mouse. The men aboard the plane were frightened, but, as one of them would later recall, LBJ wasn't. In fact, the airman remembered, Johnson was "just as calm as if he were on a sight-seeing tour."[6]

The plane managed to climb into the clouds, where the Zeros couldn't find it, and it made the flight back to the base safely. Another plane from the mission—the one LBJ had missed—was shot down; all aboard it were lost.

On his way back to the United States, LBJ stopped off in Melbourne again. Along the way the pilot got lost, wandered about, and ran out of fuel. An emergency landing had to be made, and again Johnson remained calm. Crewmen aboard that plane were impressed. When LBJ finally got to

The Senate Deal-Maker

63

Melbourne, General MacArthur gave him a Silver Star, one of the highest field awards for bravery.

So in a very official sense his campaign promise was kept. If he was a coward, he managed to conceal that fact from veteran combat flyers and from Douglas MacArthur himself. It seems more likely that LBJ wanted to be in the States to make another attempt at running for the Senate.

The Senate race that Johnson lost in 1941 almost ended his political career. He had been shocked and disappointed. He did not lose well, so even a close loss hurt. LBJ would later say of the defeat: "I felt terribly rejected, and I began to think about leaving politics and going home to make money." But the lure of small money back home didn't have the sweet aroma of the power he would possess as a Roosevelt ally in a wartime Congress.[7]

And he didn't disappoint Roosevelt. Throughout the war, Johnson rose to a strong leadership role and represented Roosevelt interests in the House. And when Roosevelt died in April of 1945, Lyndon Johnson simply became a staunch supporter of the new president, Harry S Truman.

In 1948 a Senate seat opened again, but this time it was to be a regular election; LBJ could not hold on to his seat in the House of Representatives and run for the Senate as well. He took his time deciding, but he finally jumped in and took to the campaign trail with old-fashioned energy. Recalling his defeat in his first Senate attempt, this time LBJ distanced himself from the Roosevelt and Truman administrations and painted himself as a middle-of-the-road Texan rather than as a liberal Washingtonian.

In the midst of the campaign, LBJ was hospitalized with kidney stones for about a week. After leaving the hospital, he launched into a feverish

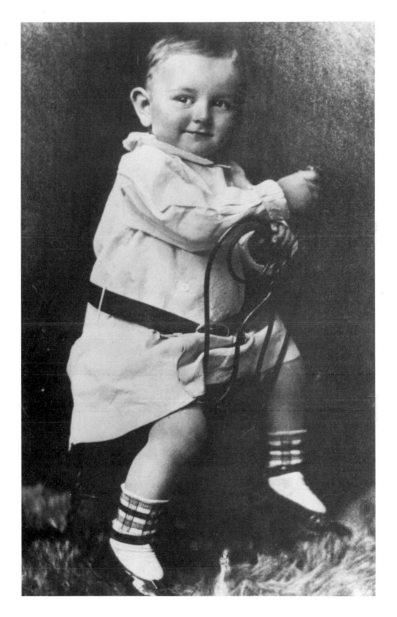

Lyndon Baines Johnson in 1910, at
eighteen months. Johnson was born in
west Texas, the oldest of five children.

Lyndon Johnson's boyhood home in Johnson
City, Texas. Johnson's father, Sam Ealy Johnson, Jr.,
is shown sitting in the rear of the car, while
Lyndon stands outside. The house is now part
of the Lyndon Baines Johnson Museum.

Lyndon Johnson (second from right) at age thirteen. He is surrounded by his siblings. Left to right: Lucia, Josefa, Rebekah, Lyndon, and Sam.

Johnson was a popular teacher and the coach of the debating team in Sam Houston High School in Houston, Texas. This 1931 picture shows Johnson (rear) with the team. Johnson was determined to win, and the trophies attest to his achievement.

Johnson with President Franklin Roosevelt in
Galveston, Texas, May 1937. Johnson had just
won his seat in Congress. During the campaign
Johnson firmly supported Roosevelt's controversial
plan to reorganize the Supreme Court.

Johnson was elected to Congress in 1937
while recuperating from an appendectomy.
Here he is shown in his hospital bed in Austin,
surrounded by congratulatory telegrams.

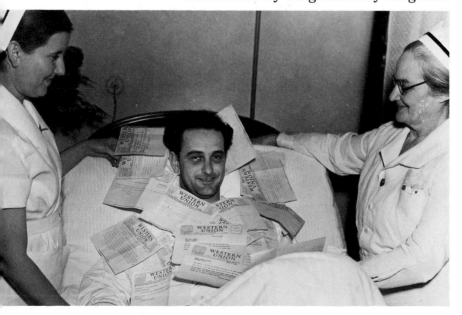

After his victory in 1937, Johnson and his
wife, Lady Bird, prepared to leave Austin for
Washington, D.C. With them are Johnson's
parents, Sam Ealy Johnson, Jr.,
and Rebekah Baines Johnson.

Johnson, held in the air by supporters during his 1941 race for the Senate. He had made powerful friends in Washington, but too few friends among Texas voters. This was the only election he ever lost, and by a scant two thousand votes.

Lt. Comdr. Lyndon Johnson of the Navy, pointing to a map of the South Pacific during World War II, 1942. Johnson had promised in a campaign speech that if he ever voted to send troops to war, he would leave his seat to go with them.

Johnson ran for the Senate again in 1948. He had learned to appeal to the voters, and is shown here campaigning with two young aides. He won the election by just eighty-seven votes.

Above: During his 1948 Senate run, Johnson made barnstorming trips across Texas in a helicopter, an aircraft few people had ever seen, building excitement with quick stops and loud speeches.

The Johnson family at the LBJ Ranch, Christmas 1952. Left to right: Lady Bird, Lucy, Lynda, and LBJ, shown with their dog Laddie.

Johnson on the floor of the Senate, 1953.
Johnson spent twelve years in the Senate
before becoming vice president in 1960.

Johnson at the Democratic National Convention, 1960,
after accepting the nomination for vice president.
Left to right: Lady Bird Johnson, Johnson, Senator
Henry Jackson of Washington, and Mrs. Jackson.

Johnson with John Kennedy during the 1960 campaign. This was the so-called Boston–Austin connection that helped the Democrats win the election from then-vice president Richard Nixon.

President John Kennedy riding in the fatal motorcade through downtown Dallas, November 22, 1963. Kennedy and Texas governor Connally were shot during the motorcade. Johnson realized that even he would be considered a suspect in the assassination.

Johnson with fellow senator Hubert Humphrey
at the Democratic National Convention in
1956. After John Kennedy's assassination in 1963,
Humphrey became Johnson's vice president.

Left: Lady Bird Johnson campaigned constantly for ecology and highway beautification. Here she is shown planting flowers in this 1965 photo.

Below: Johnson at the LBJ Ranch in November 1965. Visits to the ranch were, for the Johnsons, an idyllic time away from the troubles of Washington in the 1960s.

As part of his War on Poverty, Johnson introduced Medicare, the nation's first health insurance for the poor. Johnson is shown signing the Medicare bill in July 1965.

Johnson with Martin Luther King, Jr., in 1966. King endorsed Johnson's Great Society idea as a means of helping underprivileged blacks free themselves from life in the ghetto.

Right: Johnson used his influence with Congress to gain broad authority to continue the military action in Vietnam without officially declaring war.

Below: Vietnam War protesters outside the Pentagon in 1967. Some demonstrators carried a sign depicting Johnson as a war criminal for escalating the conflict in Vietnam.

Lyndon Johnson stunned the American public with the announcement that he would not seek reelection in 1968.

Johnson in retirement on the LBJ Ranch,
September 1972. He died at the age of
sixty-four on January 22, 1973.

campaign in which he even used a helicopter (an aircraft few people had ever seen) to make stops across Texas. He was building a sense of excitement with his quick stops and loud speeches directed against his opponent, former governor Coke Stevenson, against the rise of communism around the world, and for what he called "Peace, Preparedness and Progress."[8]

On November 3, 1948, Lyndon Baines Johnson defeated Coke Stevenson by a tiny 87-vote margin with nearly 1 million votes cast. The outcome surprised many observers because the former governor was such a popular man. Stevenson accused Johnson of vote tampering and took his case all the way to the United States Supreme Court, but a bright young Texas lawyer named Abe Fortas convinced the Court to drop the case. Fortas would one day be appointed to this same High Court by Johnson.[9]

In his biography of LBJ, Sam Houston Johnson said that the election couldn't have been fixed by either side. "If you're going to steal an election, you sure don't fool around with a piddling margin," he wrote. Of course another explanation for the close outcome may be that both sides cheated about equally, which seems more likely considering the history of both candidates.

Out of Sam Houston Johnson's own recollection we have a picture of the corrupt atmosphere in which Texas politics of the day operated. Following the outcome, the Democratic State Executive Committee met at the Commodore Perry Hotel in Austin to certify the results. As the vote was being taken, it was clear that it would be a tie: 28 to 28. Sam Houston Johnson "suddenly noticed that one of our supporters was absent. . . . Remembering that I had seen him headed for the upstairs men's room, wobbling a bit from one drink too many, I rushed into the lavatory section and found him soaking his head in a washbasin." Sam Houston Johnson says he urged the man back to the room, whereupon he voted for LBJ.[10]

What many of us would call corruption, Lyndon Johnson called plain old politics. One writer recalled of that Senate election: "I knew of the Lyndon Johnson who hired man-and-wife staff teams because, as one of his secretaries quoted him to me 'I don't want some wife at home cryin' about the cornbread gettin' cold while her husband's busy doin' somethin' for me.' Often [LBJ] drove his employees to the limits of their physical endurance or to drink. He sometimes showered staff workers with gifts, praise, and promises of greatness. He might in anger banish an employee from his sight forever, later to pay thousands of dollars for the same man's hospital bills, with no prospect of reimbursement."[11]

Despite his unpredictable behavior, Johnson had managed to make powerful allies in the House. There he had the assistance of Majority Leader Sam Rayburn and dozens of Capitol pages and assistants. But could he build a power base in a chamber where he was just one of the powerful and influential ninety-six senators?

The new senators entering that chamber with him in 1948 included future vice president Hubert H. Humphrey and a handful of men Johnson had met while in the House. But LBJ was not one to make friends in his own circle unless it suited his purposes. He liked to make friends in high places, and he was no different in the Senate.

He got himself a seat on the powerful Armed Services Committee, chaired by the widely respected Democrat from Georgia, Richard Russell.

Russell appointed LBJ chair of one subcommittee and gave him active roles on others. LBJ quickly launched into investigations of waste and corruption within the Pentagon and thus became a figure in the national news media.

Meanwhile, Johnson continued to curry the favor of powerful senators and in 1951, with the help of Humphrey and majority leader Ernest McFarland of Arizona, was voted majority whip, the number-two position in the Senate majority and an office that would help him rise to even greater power. A year later, McFarland was defeated for reelection to the Senate by Barry Goldwater, who came into office in the Dwight D. Eisenhower Republican presidential landslide. (Goldwater would later lose the presidential election to LBJ in a 1964 landslide.)[12]

McFarland, who had sponsored Johnson for the whip position, now looked to him as a possible successor in the party leadership position. (This had been transformed from majority leader to minority leader when the Republicans picked up new seats, thanks to the popularity of their presidential standard-bearer Dwight Eisenhower.)

Several of the older members of the Senate were willing to consider LBJ. But to the younger members, the Hubert Humphreys and the Eugene McCarthys, Johnson wasn't even a contender. To them, he was a peculiar, pushy outsider who spent far too much of his time in the conservative and often segregationist southern senators group. Throughout his political life, Lyndon Johnson would be regarded with suspicion by both liberals and conservatives and would often wear both of those supposedly opposite political labels at the same time.

Back home, LBJ was facing a thorny problem

along these lines. He had joined Sam Rayburn in backing Adlai Stevenson against General Dwight D. Eisenhower in the 1952 presidential election. Stevenson was a liberal—practically a communist in the eyes of Texans with a particularly conservative bent. LBJ's popularity was dwindling because of it, and Texas governor Allen Shivers was talking about running against Johnson when his seat came up in 1954.

But when Humphrey became the candidate to replace McFarland as party leader in the Senate, many conservatives became frightened and began considering LBJ. Humphrey had helped the newly developing left of the party place antisegregation planks on the 1952 presidential platform. And he had created a lot of excitement in 1948 with a similar campaign. To some, he seemed even more liberal than Stevenson.

At first, LBJ joined a group backing Richard Russell for the seat. Russell declined to run. LBJ let it be known through staff aides that he didn't like the idea of running. It would place him as the leader of the opposition party in the Eisenhower administration. Texas conservatives would not like that. Johnson sent up some smoke signals to subtly let the home-state power brokers know that he was available to be minority leader, but not without support from home. He let his brother Sam Houston Johnson be interviewed by a Dallas newspaper; Sam outlined why Lyndon didn't want to run for the minority leader seat but also insinuated that Humphrey would oppose Texas oil interests.

The ploy worked. "On and on, one call after another from powerful Texans who had read the *Dallas News* article. They were urging Lyndon to run for minority leader. . . ," Sam Houston noted.

The final straw came when Governor Shivers called to assure Lyndon that he would not try to take away his Senate seat.[13]

With the help of the Texas lobby, LBJ was unanimously nominated Senate minority leader. It must be noted that the Texas lobby was powerful, and included Sam Rayburn, who had been minority leader in the House since 1937. When Lyndon had been elected to the House, Rayburn quickly took him into his confidence. Rayburn, who lived alone in Washington and had no immediate family, appears to have virtually adopted Lyndon and Lady Bird as his own family. He became one of Lyndon's most powerful allies. Even when Lyndon went to the Senate he could rely on Rayburn's advice and political influence.[14]

If there was anything slippery about Johnson's political career, there was also something distinctive and positive about it. He was a believer in the "little people," a populist who often came to the aid of the downtrodden. And his biggest accomplishments were in the area of civil rights.

In the 1950s, both African-American and white leaders began to marshal the power of ordinary black people, campaigning to get them interested in voting and in the politics that went with voting, including the politics of racial segregation.

These actions brought the case of *Brown* v. *Board of Education of Topeka, Kansas,* to the U.S. Supreme Court, which would rule that school segregation in the South was unconstitutional. In 1955, Rosa Parks excited the imagination of the entire country when she refused to give up her seat on a Montgomery, Alabama, bus and got arrested, the arrest touching off a wave of protests. By 1957 several civil rights activists had risen to national prominence, although not to any major political positions, and the movement to gain equality for black Americans was fully under way.

The institutions first targeted for change were in the southern United States, where blacks and whites were separated from one another by law. They weren't even allowed to use the same public rest rooms. Liberal politicians from the North found it easy to attack southern racial policies, and they did so often. Southern conservatives found it equally easy to win regional elections by fighting off the liberals.

LBJ distinguished himself in this area. He had compassion for the Southerners, who he believed were not really evil but were simply mesmerized by fear of blacks.

In 1957, Johnson began to participate in the congressional fight for civil rights. The political tide was beginning to turn against the southern hardliners, and President Eisenhower had begun to speak out against some forms of racial segregation. This made it possible for a politician to be conservative and still support improvements in civil rights for blacks. For Johnson, of course, such support meant the chance to capture a broader following.

It also put him in a stronger position to defend blacks than Hubert H. Humphrey, who was perhaps the most outspoken liberal on the matter. Humphrey had little ability to sway Southerners, who were suspicious of him because of his positions favoring a stronger United Nations (which some in the southern bloc regarded as a dangerous organization) and because of his history of strong support for black civil rights. Only someone less identified with the left wing of the Democratic party, an LBJ, could bring off a legislative victory.

Oddly, the seemingly conservative Texan was beginning to impress leading Democrats with his concern for the civil rights issue and with his ability to pull together opposing political leaders to get civil rights legislation through Congress.

Johnson was the subject of conversation one spring day in 1957 at the home of liberal historian Arthur Schlesinger, Jr., an increasingly influential voice among Democrats. Schlesinger told economist (and later presidential adviser) Walt Rostow that he had been impressed with LBJ. The Texas senator had explained to Schlesinger the process of getting civil rights legislation passed. LBJ "described each member of the Senate, man by man: his constituency and problems; his biases and possibilities; how he might be moved on one issue and remain unmovable on others. The building of a Senate majority around a specific piece of legislation emerged as an intensely human task of persuasion," Rostow wrote later of that meeting.[15]

The vehicle used was the Civil Rights Act of 1957. Johnson set up the legislative debate so that Southerners could win something en route to passing the measure. Working closely with President Dwight D. Eisenhower, a conservative Republican, Johnson discouraged the Democratic majority from writing its own bill but instead got them to work on a draft document produced by the White House.

The bill included a stipulation that the federal government could send troops into any area where citizens were deprived of civil rights. It was so broad that Johnson knew the Southerners would bristle at it and throw it out. Debate over the stipulation, known as Title III, was so fierce that little attention was paid to the Civil Rights bill itself.

Throughout the skirmishing, LBJ's closest

friends advised him to remove the entire bill from consideration. They were afraid that he would lose influence with the very Southerners who had helped make him Senate leader. But Johnson managed to get the bill through. The bill that emerged was not as powerful as the civil rights legislation that was to follow, but it paved the way for that legislation and demonstrated for the first time that northern liberals and southern conservatives could be brought to a compromise over civil rights. It was, according to LBJ aide George Reedy, the future president's finest hour.[16]

As was almost always the case with LBJ, not everyone believed his finest hour to be anything more than a dramatic act of political expediency. One of the people who saw LBJ at close range in his later civil rights battles—syndicated newspaper columnist Carl T. Rowan—says he was with Johnson personally during the campaign for a sweeping civil rights bill in 1964 and was unable to firmly establish where LBJ really stood on the issue. "I think [LBJ] took pride in his personal realization that emotionally and intellectually he had grown far above his early years as a Texas congressman, or even as the Texas Senator accused of stealing an election," Rowan wrote. Rowan noted that as of 1990 there were 8,000 African-Americans holding public office in the United States. And he attributed that to a large extent to LBJ's efforts.[17]

Lynda Johnson Robb, LBJ's older daughter and wife of Virginia senator Charles Robb, recalls riding a campaign train in 1964 and encountering jeering mobs along the way. In some instances, she says, jeering anti-LBJ demonstrators openly protested his civil rights policies and threatened the First Family. The protesters were often "very mean. They would jeer and not allow us to speak."[18]

The Senate Deal-Maker

Again, LBJ was not always what he seemed. To have come so close to danger himself over civil rights suggests that he was in some way sincerely in favor of better protection of African-Americans' rights. Yet his history is deeply intertwined with the segregationist South.

In many ways LBJ was like the South of the 1960s, which was clinging to some dying traditions but also beginning to see that change was inevitable. Yet from where he stood, Lyndon Baines Johnson saw more of the American political scene than the political commentators and analysts had seen of LBJ.

But he would soon change all that.

6

Favorite
Son

National political analysts do not observe individual congressmen and even senators very closely. There are too many of them. And even in Johnson's day—before Hawaii and Alaska became states—there were ninety-six senators. So the national political watchers hadn't had a close look at LBJ yet.

But they should have noticed something about Johnson in the 1960 primary election for the Democratic presidential nomination. If the journalists who followed the campaign trail or the political scientists whose commentary appeared in important newspapers and magazines had understood the

big picture, they would have realized that Lyndon

Baines Johnson was a cloakroom politician with little appreciation for the deeper issues of statesmanship.

It was an election year, and John F. Kennedy, the young and brash senator from Massachusetts, was whistle-stopping across the country with a following of young and idealistic assistants. Stuart Symington, the older, handsome senator from Missouri, was also traveling. LBJ, the deal-maker from Texas, was staying put in Washington, expecting deals he made with other senators that summer to help him win the Democratic nomination. Aides say he would have traveled more, but he was uncertain of his appeal to a national audience and was concerned about losing influence among his fellow senators if he stayed away from them for any length of time while on the campaign trail. And there was a lot to worry about.[1]

On Capitol Hill, Johnson had fallen into an unexpected battle with an increasingly influential group of liberal labor leaders and politicians. His power as a Senate leader had been challenged by this group, and Johnson's vulnerability surprised even him. Described by *Life* magazine in July of 1960 as a "master political maneuverer," LBJ was a man who wielded immense political power, but who at the same time was unable in most instances to capture the public's imagination. He was a man who worked best behind the scenes.

Lyndon Johnson was a man of many surprises, and it has been said that he didn't fail to surprise just about everyone at the 1960 Democratic presidential nominating convention. For it was there that John F. Kennedy was nominated for president. And it was there that Kennedy offered Johnson the vice presidential slot. Supposedly, Kennedy did not expect Johnson to accept.

Kennedy, if his brother Robert has been rightly quoted, never even thought about who his running mate would be until after he was nominated. Moments later he is reported to have realized, in Robert's words, "how terrible it was that he had only twenty-four hours to select a vice president. He really hadn't thought about it at all."[2]

That may not be entirely true. Historian Arthur M. Schlesinger, Jr., notes that Kennedy had previously tried to find out if Senator Hubert H. Humphrey of Minnesota would accept the position on the ticket. Schlesinger says in his book *Robert Kennedy and His Times* that John Kennedy even approached him about Humphrey. Stuart Symington of Missouri was also reportedly under consideration. Lyndon Johnson, Schlesinger recalls, was "the one name that no one ever mentioned."

Whatever the truth of the matter, during the convention itself LBJ was key in Kennedy's nomination victory. As wrangling wore on on the convention floor, LBJ stood up for the Texas delegation and nominated Kennedy, "the fighting sailor who wears the scars of battle," to be the Democratic presidential standard-bearer.[3]

It was an important endorsement because LBJ had been an opponent of Kennedy's and a "favorite son" of Texas. Favorite sons are generally backed by their entire delegation and are supported regardless of their chances of winning the actual nomination. In other words, a favorite son candidate carries the full weight of his state's delegation, which for Texas is considerable.

LBJ also had something of a campaign victory record from the primary season. He was really the first candidate to gain any notice in the shadow of Kennedy. This happened in May after President

Eisenhower met with Soviet leader Nikita Khrushchev, an aggressive and sometimes even boisterous man, in Paris.

During the meeting, Khrushchev suddenly demanded in front of international reporters and news photographers that Eisenhower apologize for allowing a spy plane to fly over Soviet airspace. The plane, a U-2 jet aircraft, had been shot down over Russia. Eisenhower refused.

Back home, a campaigning Kennedy lashed out against President Eisenhower. He (Kennedy) wouldn't have given Khrushchev such a cold shoulder, the Massachusetts senator said. Instead, he would have expressed regret that an argument took place, a clever way of sidestepping the question of how Kennedy would have responded to the insult. Senator Johnson took a more aggressive stand: "I am not prepared to apologize to Mr. Khrushchev—are you?" he asked an audience where he was a speaker. Johnson grabbed the headlines that day and effectively launched himself into the forefront of political attention.[4]

As Senate majority leader, LBJ could bring along some powerful friends, but he also made more than a few powerful enemies. Joseph L. Rauh, Jr., a cofounder of the liberal Americans for Democratic Action (ADA) was one of them. From 1948, when Johnson entered the Senate, Rauh had clashed frequently with him over civil rights legislation, which Rauh supported far more strongly than Johnson. Johnson, in fact, fought off Rauh's attempts to change the filibuster rules, which allowed southern senators to take the Senate floor and keep it for days on end, preventing civil rights bills from being introduced.[5]

Rauh had said that the Democrats under Johnson's leadership were no different from right-wing Republicans. But he marveled that Johnson supported President Eisenhower's early civil rights bill of 1957. The bill was only a tiny step forward for African-Americans, but Johnson had to break with his fellow Southerners to provide his support. Now Rauh and the ADA were accusing Johnson of being a civil rights laggard.

It is not so much that LBJ had made a sudden change, but that the political climate was becoming more liberal. It was the dawn of an era that would place the emphasis on youth, music, and street politics. In the 1960s the strains of African-American rhythm-and-blues music and the hard beat of rock 'n' roll began to merge. Young people began to become involved in politics and were increasingly demanding a voice in the decision-making process. Television, which had not yet come to most cities in the 1950s, was now spread across the nation and was acting as a unifying factor for the up-and-coming youth culture.

It was a time in which southern moderates like Johnson were becoming more willing—but not entirely willing—to change with the tide. And it was a time when northern liberal groups like the ADA were becoming more extreme in their thinking.

If LBJ was considered by liberals to be an archconservative, he was considered by many conservatives to be an archliberal. This type of confused political identification had followed LBJ all the days of his political life, largely because he was less a statesman than a politician. A statesman has a global viewpoint that commands respect and allows him to have the last word on major issues. But a politician is a maker of compromises—one who can get both sides to give in a little in order to bring the business at hand to a conclusion. At this, Johnson was America's grand master.

A commentator in the *National Review* (a journal of conservative thought) would write that Johnson as president was "careful where his predecessor [JFK] had been flamboyant, but standing well to the left of the New Frontier." The New Frontier was Kennedy's political vision, marked by a youthful boldness and energy that launched the United States into space exploration and expanded economic opportunities on earth. It also placed a new emphasis on self-sufficiency and citizen activism. The *National Review* commentator reflected the view of most conservative thinkers that Lyndon Johnson was well to the left of John F. Kennedy.[6]

Kennedy would promise to put a man on the moon in one decade, despite the fact that at the time the United States had yet to escape earth's gravity. Kennedy made few promises but instead challenged his audiences. In one of his most celebrated speeches, he goaded his audience not to ask what their country could do for them, but to ask what they could do for their country. And he expressed a vision for world trade that would open new frontiers of product exports and imports.

Would LBJ be an asset or a liability for the Democratic ticket? Would the vice presidency be an asset or a liability for him? One friend tried to talk LBJ out of accepting the vice presidential nomination, but he reportedly answered, "Power is where power goes," a reference to his lifelong experience of taking meaningless positions and making powerful and influential jobs of them.

Something was changing in America in 1960. It was perfect for LBJ. It was the beginning of a media age in which Richard Nixon, for instance, would lose an election largely because the TV camera did not flatter him. There were serious news

Lyndon

Baines

Johnson

programs on the television networks, and millions of Americans were watching.

The media was at one of its highest points of influence, and whether he liked it or not, LBJ could see that John Kennedy had captured the hearts of the media. Running with Kennedy would put Johnson in the spotlight as well. And Kennedy was young. Johnson would be perceived as the elder statesman on the ticket. Johnson would thus get the clout he needed to run for president in the next election.[7]

Despite differences in style, and some political rhetoric that had made Johnson and JFK's younger brother Robert Kennedy adversaries for life, there were good reasons for Kennedy to select Johnson. LBJ was identified strongly with the South, where it was thought that a Roman Catholic candidate like Kennedy would have a great deal of trouble. And Kennedy had more ties to the growing new movement of the left than he had to the traditional Roosevelt Democrats. LBJ would help Kennedy gain influence with that group.

The troubles with Bobby Kennedy went to the very basic differences between LBJ and the younger Kennedy. LBJ was an organization man who liked to learn the rules and use them to his advantage. Kennedy was more of a rebel. Of his own attitude, Robert Kennedy said it best: "Some look at the condition of the world and ask why. I look at the condition of the world and ask why not."

Such a personality clash was bound to cause problems, and it did at the 1960 nominating convention. Bobby Kennedy, who was running his brother's campaign and whose Harvard University advisers were disturbed at the thought of LBJ and his southern advisers walking the halls of power, went to see LBJ, supposedly at John Kennedy's request. Bobby Kennedy asked Johnson if he didn't think his presence on the ticket would cause divisions within the party. Would LBJ care to withdraw from the vice presidential nomination? The question itself and the personality differences created the perfect background for a clash.[8]

Kennedy adviser Walt Rostow quotes JFK as saying that he and LBJ stood for the same things, but that LBJ could not get elected because he was a Southerner. This observation, while colored by whatever flaws exist in Rostow's own memory and understanding, may actually give us a key to one of the great mysteries of the 1960s. So many observers have marveled that Kennedy and Johnson were as different as night and day, and yet only Kennedy's death and Johnson's political talents could succeed in getting JFK's ideas made into institutions such as civil rights, voting rights, and space exploration. Maybe the two men were not so different after all.

When the vice presidential nomination was offered to LBJ, Johnson quickly consulted with Sam Rayburn and Richard Russell, who counseled against taking it. But Kennedy himself called on Rayburn to press Johnson to change his mind. How ironic it was that Kennedy told Rayburn, "Lyndon would be the most qualified man for the Presidency if anything should happen to me."[9]

Kennedy assured Rayburn and then Johnson himself that LBJ would play an important role in the Kennedy White House. Not only would he be the administration's "point man" on major projects, but he would spearhead all of the Kennedy administration's efforts to get bills passed in Congress.

A political point man, like his counterpart in the military, is expected to go out ahead of his associates and look for unexpected dangers. While his position was politically dangerous—in that he would have to tangle personally with opposition members of Congress when Kennedy wanted to introduce a bill—Johnson could handle it and could increase his power among the legislators. This was something that LBJ could understand. He accepted the vice presidential nomination.

The response was immediate and positive. The week after the convention, *Time* magazine noted: "Johnson's unexpected presence on the Kennedy Democratic ticket upset a basic assumption of [Richard] Nixon's campaign strategy. To offset advantages that Kennedy's New England origin and Roman Catholicism will give him in the East, Nixon had hoped to win a clutch of electoral votes in the South, capturing at least four states— Florida, Tennessee, Texas and Virginia—that Dwight Eisenhower captured in both 1952 and 1956. By dimming Nixon's prospects in the South, the Kennedy-Johnson ticket confronted him with a tough problem in electoral vote arithmetic. Even if Nixon can overcome farmer discontent and carry the farm belt, he cannot win the election unless he can beat Kennedy in some of the big industrial states east of the Missippi." Even the traditionally Republican farm belt would now be in doubt partly because of Johnson's farming heritage.[10]

Not to be overlooked was Johnson's association with the "Bible Belt," the geographic part of the country generally regarded as encompassing an area stretching from the Mississippi Valley to the southeastern United States, Texas, and Louisiana. In the Bible Belt, people took the Bible seriously. They even established Bible colleges. Methodists, Baptists, and Presbyterians led the area in its thinking. Religious fundamentalism, which believes that the Bible is literally true, had a profound effect on the people of this region, as to a large extent it still does today.

This was extremely important if the Democrats were going to put up a Roman Catholic presidential candidate. They had tried it unsuccessfully with New York governor Al Smith a generation before. The southern wing of the Democratic party and many Republicans were not ready for a Catholic. They were fearful of undue influence on such a president by the pope, the head of the Roman Catholic Church.

On September 9, 1960, a group of Protestant clergymen led by Norman Vincent Peale of New York's Marble Collegiate Church, issued a statement in Washington expressing their concern about the influence the pope might have over Kennedy.[11]

How much could LBJ, with his Bible Belt heritage, help Kennedy through this? A few days later, the running mates were together at the Alamo in San Antonio, Texas. Picket signs said, "We don't want the Kremlin and the Vatican." Johnson made a speech that was to become a standard of the 1960 campaign. It basically recounted how during World War II Kennedy had commanded a patrol boat in the Pacific. The boat was sunk when it was rammed by a Japanese destroyer. "And when he was savin' those American boys that was in his crew," Johnson said, "they didn't ask what church he belonged to."[12]

Here was Lyndon Baines Johnson at his best, playing the role of political hero to Kennedy's outcast, just as he had done at San Marcos when he organized all the outsiders to form the White Stars. Just the way he would do it as he surprised a nation that observed his unique vice presidency.

Mr.
Vice President

No one outside the administration expected Lyndon Johnson to do much as vice president. It was, in the view of many, a nothing job. Since the foundation of the United States, the vice presidency had been looked upon even by some of its officeholders as only a title. In December of 1793, Vice President John Adams wrote to his wife, Abigail: "My country has in its wisdom contrived for me the most insignificant office that ever the invention of man contrived or his imagination conceived. . . ."[1]

Adams had never met Lyndon Johnson.

Johnson was John F. Kennedy's man behind

the scenes. LBJ worked the corridors of the Senate as if he had never left, power-swapping with the great leaders of the legislative branch of government to smooth the way for JFK's executive decisions. He often came close to arranging compromises for the Kennedy legislative program, but failed more often than not because he had to work against some of JFK's own aides, including JFK's brother Robert, who openly despised LBJ. But work he did.

If the two had been at odds before the 1960 election, winning seemed to make things worse. Bobby, with his contempt for the established order in Washington, D.C., became personally entangled with J. Edgar Hoover, the powerful and sometimes treacherous director of the Federal Bureau of Investigation. Hoover only reluctantly acted to carry out the orders of the Attorney General's Office run by Bobby—especially those orders that enforced civil rights policies.

Bobby Kennedy began leaking stories to the press about FBI blunders and intimated to reporters, off the record, that Hoover was paranoid and mean-spirited as well as very dangerous.[2]

Hoover, who had known LBJ for years, asked him to get Bobby Kennedy to back away from his belligerent position. Johnson went to John Kennedy and tried to smooth over the relationship. Bobby Kennedy perceived this as a personal attack by LBJ, and to some extent he was correct. And LBJ, who had always felt uneasy around intellectuals and academicians, felt especially uneasy around Bobby, who surrounded himself with such people.

Despite the tensions between LBJ and Bobby, John Kennedy would use Johnson as a close adviser on a range of issues, including space and farm policy. Much of what the young president got from his older vice president will never be brought out in public because the two held frequent private meetings, something not too many vice presidents do with their presidents.

Kennedy, presidential adviser Walt Rostow said, ". . . took extraordinary pains to keep the vice president informed. For example, Kennedy rescheduled a major item on the agenda in a foreign policy meeting because Johnson's plane was late."[3]

As he had been in his Senate years, Johnson was a staunch proponent of America's new space program, and Kennedy publicly referred to Johnson as the man who ran the space program for the administration. To most people, this was just another example of a president putting his vice president away into an obscure corner. But Lyndon Johnson was a man who loved obscure corners as places where he could build power bases without any interference. This was just another case of Lyndon Johnson running errands in the center of power so that he could create opportunities for himself.

To casual observers, putting LBJ in charge of the space program when the U.S. had nothing to launch and no one to launch it was laughable. But to a careful observer it might have been clear that LBJ had built for himself a group of supporters within the Defense Department who kept him closely posted on the future of space exploration and on space developments in the Soviet Union.

Johnson and his Senate Preparedness Subcommittee in 1957 had begun looking into a "missile gap" between the United States and the Soviet Union. LBJ hired Cyrus Vance as special counsel and started a detailed and lengthy investigation into America's preparedness for space. Johnson called the missile gap a threat to national security —which it was to those who felt America needed to have at least as effective an arsenal of missiles as the Soviets to ensure against a preemptive Soviet attack on American targets.

Johnson proposed that the U.S. set a course for reaching milestones in the exploration of space and that a timetable be set for sending an American to the moon. Later, Kennedy would make his proposal to place an American on the moon within a decade, but it was LBJ who laid the groundwork.[4]

In his book *The Right Stuff,* journalist Tom Wolfe recorded Johnson's movements on a day when pioneer astronaut John Glenn was to be launched into space:

> A few blocks away, on a quaint Arlington side street, in a limousine, waits Lyndon Johnson, Vice-President of the United States. . . . Johnson, like many men who have had the job of Vice-President before him, has begun suffering from publicity deprivation. He decides he wants to go inside the Glenn household and console Annie Glenn [the astronaut's wife] over the ordeal, the excruciating pressure of the five-hour wait and the frustrating [launch] cancellation. To make this sympathy call all the more memorable, Johnson decides it would be nice if he brought NBC-TV, CBS-TV and ABC-TV along with him, in the form of a pool crew who will feed the touching scene to all three networks and out to the millions. The only rub—the only rub, to Johnson's way of thinking—is that he wants the *Life* [magazine] reporter, [Loudon] Wainwright, to get out of the house, because his presence will antagonize the rest of the print

reporters who can't get in, and they will not think kindly of the Vice President.

Mrs. Glenn had no desire to go on national television. She had a severe speech impediment—she stammered. After talking to her husband on the phone, Mrs. Glenn decided to keep Johnson out of her home, an act that infuriated the vice president. He later got to play host to all the astronauts at a very well-known party opening the new Apollo space center in Johnson's home state. The vice president may have been kept out of the Glenn home on one important occasion, but he would bring the entire space program to his home state at a later date.

Maybe he was moved into a not very visible position when Kennedy made him the administration's executive in charge of the space program, but he used the obscure position to garner tremendous power. We may even doubt whether Kennedy actually moved him out of the way. Johnson, of course, wielded tremendous influence on Capitol Hill, especially in the Senate, where as vice president of the United States he served as president pro tem, an office that gave him the tie-breaking vote.

Johnson was, however, in general sold a bill of goods on how much power he would wield for the Kennedy administration on Capitol Hill. When Kennedy approached LBJ to run with him, he convinced LBJ that his experience as Senate majority leader would be put to work. But once in office, Kennedy turned more to his brother Robert and a group of liberal young politicians to push legislative programs. It was a mistake that would cost Kennedy a lot of support on Capitol Hill. It would also embitter the newly elected vice president, Johnson.

"The Kennedys had easy access to the greatest legislative strategist of this century—Lyndon Johnson—but they refused to use him," Sam Houston Johnson complained. "Instead there was a swarm of young, conceited New Frontiersmen running around Capitol Hill trying to tell elderly Congressmen 'This is the way it's going to be.'" The old guard was put off by these upstarts, and LBJ was part of the old guard.[5]

Writing after his brother's death, Sam Houston Johnson said that LBJ felt particularly humiliated by that tactic. In fact, Sam said he himself stayed away from Washington throughout most of LBJ's vice presidency because "I didn't want to be a firsthand witness to my brother's day-to-day humiliation."

But Kennedy trusted Johnson with some very delicate negotiations, possibly because Johnson was such an adept back-room dealer. Kennedy sent him and Lady Bird—along with Kennedy's brother-in-law Stephen Smith and his wife, Jean, Kennedy's sister—on a presidential jet to meet Ngo Dinh Diem in Saigon in May of 1961.[6]

Johnson and Smith were to present Kennedy's plans for supporting the Diem government with military and financial aid. This may have looked like another case of LBJ running mere errands, but he was actually sent in anticipation that Diem would not like the Kennedy proposals and would want to discuss them with a powerful individual—LBJ.

Talking had always been LBJ's strong point. He could work the halls of Congress or a large political rally with admirable skill. Presidential adviser Walt Rostow, who had written many speeches on

Lyndon

Baines

Johnson

foreign policy and had advised JFK on foreign policy issues, was impressed with the strength of a foreign policy speech Vice President Johnson made before the Advertising Council. Rostow heard LBJ defend Kennedy's growing use of foreign aid. Rostow calls it "the most effective speech in support of foreign aid I had ever heard."[7]

One of the major areas in which LBJ was to help the Kennedy administration was in relations with farming interests. The Democratic party platform plank on "the farm issue" called for the expanded consumption of farm goods at home. It also called for the food-stamp program that LBJ would eventually bring into existence.

In the 1960 election, JFK was quoted as saying, "No domestic issue is more important in this election than the farm issue. No part of the American way of life is more important—or more in trouble—than the family farm." Those were tough words from a senator from Boston who had no connection with farming people. Clearly, LBJ, the owner of a Texas ranch and the son of farmers and ranchers, would add farm-belt luster to Kennedy's campaign. The farm belt also would become LBJ's concern in the presidential years.[8]

But LBJ's biggest vice presidential triumph came in his appointment as chairman of the President's Committee on Equal Employment Opportunity. Here he was able to craft important regulatory power among a new and rapidly growing constituency: African-Americans. The post had been created in the Eisenhower administration to keep then vice president Richard Nixon busy. Unfortunately, Nixon's committee accomplished virtually nothing.

But LBJ was going to be different. He hired his friend and legal counsel Abe Fortas to help draft an

90

executive order John Kennedy would have to sign. In essence, it would force contractors who made money from the federal government to sign a document certifying that they did not practice racial discrimination.[9]

In this he did Kennedy a favor because the president was having little success in getting Congress to give him civil rights legislation. LBJ knew how to circumvent Congress when he had to, and in this instance it proved to be a success—briefly.

The vice president also knew that Congress would not appropriate money for his office to enforce the new executive order. So he began to go to Cabinet departments to talk them out of small stipends, thus thwarting the anticipated will of Congress.[10]

Members of Johnson's committee quickly became troubled by his methods. And some senior members of Congress were disturbed by the fact that the committee seemed to thrive without any funding. The committee ran into more trouble when Bobby Kennedy learned that it had done virtually nothing to enforce the executive order at NASA, the new space agency over which LBJ had so much power. Bobby, in front of the whole committee, derided LBJ for his lack of progress; that brought the work of the committee to a standstill.

To liberal observers, including union leader Walter Reuther, LBJ's actions seemed peculiar, and seemed to be aimed at preventing progress. Little could anyone know that LBJ would one day create the Equal Employment Opportunity Commission (EEOC), viewed by liberal commentators as a progressive idea.[11]

Even before LBJ became president, when he had organized the Plan for Progress, he had shown himself to be more than a talker on the issue of equal opportunity for black Americans. The Plan for Progress was a loosely organized confederacy of volunteer corporations that had agreed to fulfill the executive order guidelines in hiring minorities. By November of 1963, 104 companies were in the group.[12]

While LBJ plotted and planned, President Kennedy built a strong relationship with the national media. Kennedy's wife was glamorous, he himself was athletic and exciting, and his world included globe-hopping diplomacy and touch football on the White House lawn. Kennedy was the darling of the media, and they dubbed his White House "Camelot." While this promoted the idea that Kennedy was a knight in shining armor surrounded by valiant men and virtuous ladies, it did little to get any of his programs passed through Congress. Two years into his presidency, Kennedy was frustrated at the resistance he was meeting from Congress and he was worrying about his own political future. Reelection was beginning to loom on the horizon, and public opinion polls showed that Kennedy needed to get out on the campaign trail again, especially in areas of the nation that had been pro-Nixon in 1960.

Once again, Texas was a crucial swing state and Kennedy had to win there. With the help of Vice President Johnson and Texas governor John Connally, a longtime LBJ friend, Kennedy was about to embark on a trip to Texas in the hope of convincing conservative Texas voters that Camelot had something for them as well as for brash young Easterners.

8

The Death
of JFK

 The delicate political work of art that had been woven into Camelot was shattered in an instant. The assassin's bullet that took the life of President John F. Kennedy at once brought the entire dream to a halt.

Kennedy, accompanied by LBJ and Texas governor John Connally, had visited Dallas on that crisp November morning to help strengthen his weak image in the politically important state of Texas. Kennedy was fighting with Congress and was perceived by many traditional Democrats as someone who simply did not fit in. He needed a political boost.

LBJ himself recalled that Kennedy was concerned about the upcoming reelection campaign. Johnson quotes JFK as saying on the morning of the assassination: "We're going to carry two states next year if we don't carry any others: Massachusetts and Texas."[1]

Indeed, the trip to Texas, and to Dallas in particular, was in many ways a calculated risk. Kennedy was not at the height of his popularity, and LBJ said of Dallas that it had "never been exactly a citadel of Democratic politics . . . but Dallas put on a different face on the afternoon of November 22, a smiling, happy, festive face eager to do honor to its president and his lady and to make them feel welcome."[2]

The needed boost would be a triumphal tour of Texas, accompanied by the most powerful local politicians. Mrs. Johnson rode in an open car with the vice president and Senator Ralph Yarborough. They waved energetically at the thousands who lined the streets of Dallas that autumn day. Suddenly, Lady Bird heard the explosion of a gunshot. Pandemonium broke out. The Kennedys rode in the first car in the motorcade. The Connallys were in the car with them. The Johnsons and Yarborough were next. A voice came over the radio in the Johnson car: "Let's get out of here!" Secret Service agent Rufus Youngblood jumped over the front seat of the open limo and jumped on top of Vice President Johnson. Mrs. Johnson recalled that she and Yarborough ducked and didn't sit up again until they arrived at Parkland Hospital, where President Kennedy would be pronounced dead.[3]

In the days that followed the assassination, accusations flew in every direction. The alleged assassin himself, Lee Harvey Oswald, was captured quickly. But while being transferred from one holding pen to another, Oswald was shot to death by Jack Ruby, a nightclub owner and friend of gangsters. Who were these people? Were they on their own or were they working with others? How could the president be gunned down in Johnson territory? Johnson recognized that even he was a suspect in the heinous crime.[4]

LBJ wasted no time in organizing a commission to investigate the assassination. Supreme Court chief justice Earl Warren would become its chairman, and the commission would function under his name. Warren is said to have been against the commission and against his own appointment for largely constitutional reasons. He knew "that it was not a good precedent to involve the Supreme Court in such an investigation." He felt too close to Kennedy and to all those who were closest to the president to be an objective judge. But LBJ prevailed upon him to take it.[5]

The commission didn't submit a final report until September 24, 1964, and then left many questions unanswered in the public mind. Lee Harvey Oswald, who was never convicted in court of murdering Kennedy, was regarded as the lone gunman, a theory challenged by many commentators. What about the fact that Oswald had lived in Russia and had been given a dishonorable discharge from the United States Marines? What about Jack Ruby, the man who shot Oswald to death before the accused assassin could be brought to trial, and Ruby's connections to the underworld, particularly mobsters with former connections to Cuba? Was there a wider plot? This question is still unanswered, but LBJ had conducted himself with honor and was never seriously considered a suspect.[6]

On the day of the assassination, Johnson

went to the presidential plane after leaving the hospital. He had not been injured. Secret Service agents and Texas state police joined him as he boarded the plane at Love Field in Dallas. He waited there patiently until Mrs. Kennedy arrived, accompanying her husband's body. Federal District Judge Sarah T. Hughes met the plane and swore Johnson in as thirty-sixth president of the United States right there in Dallas.[7]

In a matter of hours and days, LBJ became a rock-solid symbol of fatherly stability. He held back from moving into the White House, giving Mrs. Kennedy time to get her life in order. He appointed the Warren Commission. And then he went to work on Congress.

The first months of the Lyndon Johnson presidency were tailor-made for him. Here was LBJ the hardworking back-room deal-maker standing in the midst of the calamity caused by the death of Kennedy. All eyes were on him. Just as he had stepped into the father role when his own father had gone off to Austin, just as he revitalized the Little Congress when it had become irrelevant to anything, suddenly LBJ was thrust into the role of loyal knight appointed to protect the realm following the death of modern Camelot's own Arthur—JFK.

This was a moment of opportunity for Lyndon the deal-maker. Now all those bills—the Civil Rights Act, a major tax bill, and several pieces of daring social legislation—were coming up for votes. Kennedy could not have gotten them through Congress, but this was LBJ's turf.

"Kennedy's legislative record is substantial, notably so if one includes measures put by him to Congress, but not passed until after his death," wrote presidential adviser (to both Kennedy and Johnson) Walt Rostow. ". . . It is clear that the massive legislative revolution of the 1960s took place during Lyndon Johnson's presidency."[8]

This was Johnson's finest hour. He would bring the nation together, prove once and for all that he was the man to wield awesome power, and place his personal stamp upon a platform Kennedy had constructed. America, Johnson hoped, would soon forget JFK and warmly embrace LBJ as president.

Still, Kennedy's Camelot was viewed even by the most hard-bitten critics as real. Just as King Arthur dwelled admirably in the ancient Camelot of fiction, JFK dwelled with the "best and the brightest advisers" in the White House. He was the very image of a legendary leader, filled with the wisdom and strength of a bygone day.

Even death didn't change that. His death was to be treated as one of the great moments of U.S. history. White House chief usher J. B. West later recalled that Mrs. Kennedy ordered JFK's funeral to be patterned after that of Abe Lincoln, an obvious touch meant to conjure up venerable images of another assassinated, and great, president.[9]

In the beginning it was not the public that Johnson had to win over so much as it was the Congress and the Cabinet. These were the people who had to believe he could handle the transition into the presidency. One month after the Kennedy assassination Johnson called a meeting of advisers to discuss the upcoming State of the Union address.

"Three geological layers . . . of Johnson's advisers were there: friends from the longer past, Clark Clifford, Abe Fortas and James Rowe; Kennedy men, including McGeorge Bundy and Theodore Sorensen; and his [LBJ's] emerging new staff . . . ," according to Walt Rostow.

Johnson noted that he spoke with a drawl and

should make the State of the Union speech shorter because he took longer to speak. He spoke of a need to deal with Vietnam. He discussed getting more support for aid to Latin America. He vowed to move ahead with an antipoverty program. He wanted to shift resources from the military to education and welfare (an apparent contradiction with his desire to resolve the Vietnam issue—a contradiction that would hurt his presidency later).

The effect of this meeting, Rostow reports, was to reinforce his (Rostow's) pleasure in staying on with Johnson after Kennedy's death, undoubtedly the reason for the meeting.[10]

Where Kennedy had encouraged the image of a Camelot, a magic kingdom over which Jackie ruled as queen, Johnson walked the White House with a clumsy style that drove White House workers insane.

J. B. West, then chief usher of the White House, reports that Johnson didn't like the way the presidential shower worked. LBJ supposedly sent West packing to The Elms, the home the Johnson family used during his vice presidential days, to see how LBJ's "multinozzle" shower worked. West had the White House shower rebuilt at what he says was a cost of "thousands of dollars" to suit LBJ's taste in bathing.

"Taste" was a word that had become so important during the Kennedy years. Mrs. Kennedy once used network television to take the nation on a tour of the White House. There she showed off paintings, furniture, and designs that were the marks of a very tasteful First Lady. And JFK was seen as a fashionable man himself, so that style was everywhere in the White House.

When LBJ took over, talk about style in the
White House came to a sudden halt. Lady Bird,

although less the woman of the world than Mrs. Kennedy seemed to be, was capable and gracious in public. If the spotlight had been on her alone, then the Johnson White House would not have seemed so clumsy in comparison with the Kennedy White House.

It was LBJ himself who brought a new and lowbrow atmosphere to the place. For instance, Johnson created a national guffaw and a stir when he opened his shirt to reveal a surgical scar to press photographers. And he embarrassed many of his staff aides and scores of commentators when on April 27, 1964, he picked a beagle up by the ears right in front of news photographers.[11]

The Johnsons tried to move gracefully from their vice presidential quarters to the White House, giving Mrs. Kennedy extra time to pull her effects together and leave. The Kennedys would intimate to friends that Mrs. Kennedy had been rushed, but White House aides said the Johnsons gave her more time than anyone expected.

Moving the Johnson family into the White House was an unexpected revelation to all involved. Luci, the younger Johnson girl at age sixteen, took John-John Kennedy's old room, and the bedroom once occupied by Caroline Kennedy was now Lynda's room whenever she returned from college. She was nineteen at the time. For young Luci, the move was a step into a strange mixture of freedom and celebrity. Luci, for instance, noticed the phone at her bedside and asked the White House chief usher if it was a direct line or an extension. At home, LBJ had listened in on her telephone calls. Here at the White House, to Luci's delight, her phone was her own. He would no longer be listening in on her private calls.

For Lady Bird, finding privacy was no easy

task. She took over a tiny dressing room in the southwest corner of the White House second floor to record in her diary. "I loved that room," she said. "I put my own furniture in it—my blue velvet sofa from the Elms. The back of it is faded from the sun that streamed into the southwest window."[12]

For the next five years, the Johnson family would struggle to maintain some semblance of Texas family life and some semblance of normalcy. On January 17, 1964, Lady Bird made a poignant entry in her diary: "Luci Baines came in from school just as I was about to bid [some guests] good-by, her arms full of books, old tennis shoes, and coats, wailing about finals, so I think [the guests] must have realized we were a fairly normal family." Living in a fishbowl was difficult for the Johnsons.

In some senses, the Johnsons were a perfectly normal 1960s family. Their teenage daughters listened to rock 'n' roll, spent hours on the telephone, and dated young men their parents didn't like. At eighteen, Luci Johnson was far more trouble than her older sister, Lynda. Just as Lady Bird had changed the spelling of her nickname from Bird to Byrd, Lucy Johnson changed her name unofficially from Lucy to Luci and actually persuaded White House reporters to use the new spelling. Such antics made Lyndon Johnson uneasy, although Mrs. Johnson would write in her diary that she approved of the name change.[13]

But there were aspects of public life that strained the Johnson household. Luci acknowledged to reporters that she resented the way LBJ took Lady Bird away to political affairs. She once screamed and stomped her feet as her parents left the White House for a political rally.[14]

For Lynda, the move to the White House was also a strange mixture of challenges. She came home from the University of Texas because LBJ and Lady Bird wanted the family together for this auspicious period of their lives. "I liked my independence to plan my own schedule," Lynda recalls. "I thought I would feel very lonely [in the White House]." Lady Bird accepted that argument and allowed Lynda to move into the White House with a college friend, Warrie Lynn Smith, who belonged to the same sorority Lynda had joined.[15]

Apart from settling family issues, LBJ's biggest challenge was to wield the power he had gathered while in Congress without seeming to erase the image of the late President Kennedy. Johnson was especially sensitive about the media. He had several televisions in the Oval Office, for instance, and constantly watched network news to see a reflection of himself in the TV coverage. The media generally perceived him as a Southerner, a conservative, and quite the opposite of JFK.

Johnson worked hard to overcome that image. On December 2, 1963, he publicly alienated the three Republican members of the Atomic Energy Commission (AEC) by presenting to Dr. Robert Oppenheimer the Enrico Fermi Award for excellence in science. Oppenheimer had been director of the project to build America's first atom bomb during World War II. But he had later expressed liberal opinions and was seen by powerful anticommunists as a communist himself. Oppenheimer had been blacklisted, meaning he could no longer find work as a scientist because of his political beliefs.

Oppenheimer, who had associated with socialist and other leftist students in California before World War II, had taken a more neutral political position as he led a group of the world's leading physicists in building the first atomic bombs, which they had expected would be used against the Nazi German government, an extreme right-wing dictatorship. But by the time the bomb was ready for use, the Nazis had surrendered and the bombs were used against Japan. Shortly after World War II, Oppenheimer criticized American foreign policy and even questioned the use of two atom bombs against Japan. At the same time, an anticommunist fervor was sweeping the nation, and Oppenheimer was among those identified by later discredited Senator Joseph McCarthy as an enemy of the United States. McCarthy's investigation ruined Oppenheimer's career.

President Kennedy, who had wanted to put an official end to the era of blacklisting, nominated Oppenheimer for the award. With Kennedy dead only a short while, LBJ had ample excuse to cancel the ceremony and let the subject fade away. But he chose to go through with it, and it was taken as a signal that he would continue in the spirit Kennedy imparted to the White House. The three ranking Republicans on the Atomic Energy Commission boycotted the ceremony.[16]

Actually, LBJ had little choice but to go through with the award. Indeed, he was taking great pains to ease any fears that he would steer a radically different course. People don't like change, so certain things would not be done differently. Johnson, immediately after Kennedy's death, sought to retain the Kennedy Cabinet. He wrote:

> Naturally, all the Cabinet members were deeply shaken by President Kennedy's death. But apart from the Attorney General [Robert Kennedy] few of them had been close to him before 1961. The effect on the White House staff was quite another matter. Many of them

had been with Jack Kennedy since his early days in Congress. His loss was the deepest kind of tragedy to them. . . .[17]

Johnson thought any move by Cabinet members to leave would be taken by the watchful international community as a sign of his administration's weakness. More surprising to Johnson was the fact that so many White House aides stayed on. He knew they didn't particularly like him. They were doing it out of a sense of loyalty to the country. Johnson noted that Theodore Sorenson stayed on the White House staff until March 1964, serving as a presidential adviser and helping to smooth the transition to a Johnson White House. He resigned to write a history of the Kennedy administration. Arthur Schlesinger, an international affairs adviser, also stepped down to write a book. Pierre Salinger, the White House press secretary under Kennedy, resigned to run for the Senate in California. Salinger won the Democratic primary but lost the election. Since Salinger won the primary, when the incumbent senator, Clair Engle, died, Salinger was appointed by the California governor to complete the term.

McGeorge Bundy remained, and actually became a close confidant of Johnson's. So did Lawrence O'Brien, who remained as a legislative aide and later became Johnson's postmaster general and a Democratic national chairman. (O'Brien went on to become commissioner of the National Basketball Association.)

Johnson's sheer energy kept the old White House system going. Former White House usher J. B. West called Johnson the "perpetual motion president." He would rise at 6 A.M. and read two or three newspapers while making phone calls. By

8 A.M. he'd be having breakfast in bed with Lady Bird.

Johnson would be at his desk by 9 A.M. and wouldn't break again for lunch until 3 P.M. Unexpected guests were constantly brought into the White House dining room at all hours of the day and night.

One thing that remained forever the same was Johnson's image as a Texan. Everything had to be bigger than life to make it real. Yet everything had to be homespun. On Christmas morning in 1963, the Johnsons were home at their ranch. Early in the morning Mrs. Johnson got in the car and personally delivered poinsettias to her neighbors. She loved to take drives "over the beautiful Hill Country which I loved so much."

Mrs. Johnson's love for the countryside and her constant campaigns for highway beautification and ecology helped enhance Johnson's image among liberals. Her style helped offset some of his seemingly oafish ways. She was careful of the environment and the people around her.

Lyndon liked to ride, and even speed, around the ranchlands in a car, but his favorite mode of transportation was horseback and he liked to have a few of "the guys" along for the ride. Many newspaper reporters and Cabinet members developed calluses from visiting the LBJ ranch and joining the president in his rides.

These were idyllic jaunts away from the troubles of Washington and away from the noise and cares of a big city. Here you could sit atop a horse and look out at a vast expanse of land just as LBJ's ancestors had done a century earlier. The raucous 1960s were far from this place.

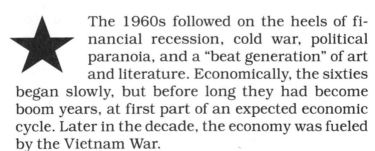

9

The 1960s:
The Great
Society

The 1960s followed on the heels of financial recession, cold war, political paranoia, and a "beat generation" of art and literature. Economically, the sixties began slowly, but before long they had become boom years, at first part of an expected economic cycle. Later in the decade, the economy was fueled by the Vietnam War.

The previous decade had seen the real beginnings of an African-American civil rights movement, particularly in the southern states, where civil rights marches were being organized to protest racist policies such as segregation. The Cold **105**

War was under way, and the fears of nuclear war that came with it. Jet planes were thundering in the air, shrinking the parameters of the globe.

On October 4, 1957, the Soviet Union embarrassed the United States by launching the first vehicle into space, a satellite named *Sputnik.* This kicked off the space race, with America the loser in the first few years. The nation's Vanguard rocket program was a failure, and while the Russians were preparing to go to the moon, the United States could barely dream of launching a rocket that could take off successfully and consistently.

America, which had rebuilt Europe and Japan through the Marshall Plan and other postwar reconstruction projects, was now facing stiff competition from both areas in the international marketplace. America's knack for bringing new and better products to market was suddenly being challenged by Japan, West Germany, and several other nations. The United States was ripe for something new, and one of the signals of that phenomenon was to be the election of John F. Kennedy.

So when Lyndon Johnson was thrust into the presidency by Kennedy's sudden death, the Texan was under almost immediate pressure to carry on the Camelot "tradition." Johnson's politics were sunk deeply in Franklin D. Roosevelt's New Deal, the name given to a 1930s package of programs designed to help restore the American economy after years of vast unemployment, inflation, and financial depression. The New Deal created about forty-five social programs.

It made sense for Johnson to handle the challenge of the 1960s in a similar way. He needed a campaign, a battle strategy whose very name would bring up images of strength and federal generosity and vision. Thus was the Great Society born.

Actually, the seed for the Great Society was not of LBJ's planting. It was a Kennedy idea. It was called the War on Poverty, and it was meant to be a comprehensive plan for dealing with the root causes of poverty in America. Before his death, Kennedy had ordered the White House Council of Economic Advisers to devise such a plan. On the first full day of his presidency, LBJ was approached by the council's chairman, Walter Heller, and asked what should be done. "Go ahead. Give it the highest priority. Push ahead full tilt," Johnson responded.[1] He was looking ahead to his own race for the White House in the next year. The Great Society would be more than a program to stimulate the American imagination—it would be a platform for a presidential candidate. In fact, Johnson probably ensured that the Great Society would win congressional approval by his choice of running mate in the 1964 presidential election.

There had, of course, been some discussion of choosing Attorney General Robert Kennedy, the late president's brother. But Johnson clearly would not tolerate that. He and RFK had never gotten along, and LBJ considered him a handicap. At best he would help stir up memories of the JFK White House. Instead, Johnson selected Senator Hubert H. Humphrey of Minnesota. Humphrey, a liberal, had joined the Senate the same year as LBJ. They had become cloakroom friends.[2]

Humphrey had been an outspoken civil rights advocate and would bring farm and industrial votes to the campaign. As LBJ had been JFK's man in charge of space, Humphrey could easily become LBJ's man in charge of health, education, and welfare. It was an easy choice—Hubert Humphrey would be Johnson's Great Society man.

If the Great Society suffered from anything, it was the Johnsonian knack for excess. In the beginning the program was meant to rectify several injustices affecting minorities and poor people. Over decades they had been systematically excluded from the good life that had marked America after World War II. The point of the program "was to make ignorance, mental retardation, ill health, and even ugliness illegal," according to former senator Eugene McCarthy, who challenged Johnson for the presidency in 1968.[3]

Layer upon layer of bureaucracy was added to the federal government until over 400 federally sponsored programs, agencies, and task forces were assembled. Johnson even established the new Cabinet posts of secretary of housing and urban development and secretary of transportation.

LBJ was bitter about the way this bureaucracy had suddenly grown. He said later that he had never intended it to become so complex. Actually, Johnson—along with most other observers of the mid-1960s—sensed that the nation was fragmented over political and economic issues, not to mention the war in Vietnam. He was striving, Johnson said, to draw the disparate parties together in some sort of national consensus.

"Unfortunately, the word 'consensus' came to be profoundly misunderstood," Johnson noted. "What consensus meant to some people was a search for the lowest common denominator. . . . To me consensus meant, first, deciding what needed to be done regardless of the political implications, and second, convincing a majority of the Congress and the American people of the necessity for doing these things."[4]

Without meaning to do so, LBJ clearly underscored the main problem with his presidency. He was the ultimate deal-maker. He was the man who went behind the scenes and brought powerful parties together. He had never been an executive long enough to develop the decision-making prowess needed to run any organization—especially a country. An executive executes. A deal-maker makes deals.

Whatever its faults, the Great Society was an answer to some of the bloody questions plaguing the United States in the 1960s. And many of the issues went right to LBJ's marrow. At the beginning of the decade, the African-American struggle for equality focused mainly on the southern states, where official segregation, or separation of the races, was practiced. And where those in power were mostly white and those out of power were mostly black.

Blacks in the South had many economic disadvantages compared with whites and even with a small but growing number of northern blacks. But the southern blacks held certain advantages. One, ironically, was the result of racial segregation. Southern blacks belonged in large numbers to all-black churches and attended all-black schools and colleges. There arose among them an intellectually gifted and determined leadership including labor-union leader Bayard Rustin and church leader Martin Luther King, Jr.

The rising black leadership (Negro leadership, as it was then called) favored nonviolent means of getting their points across. By the summer of 1960, sit-ins were the most common form of protest against segregationist policies. At these political demonstrations, blacks would sit at luncheon counters where only whites were allowed and would refuse to move until arrested, or they would

109

sit in the lobbies of buildings where they were not welcome until escorted to jails by club-wielding police. So dramatically did they make their point that the Democratic presidential platform of 1960 specifically approved of sit-ins, and both presidential candidates—Republican Richard Nixon and Democrat John Kennedy—endorsed this form of protest.[5]

In August of 1965 young black people took to the streets of Watts, the Los Angeles ghetto, snarling at police over an alleged act of brutality against an arrested black man. They shouted antigovernment and antiwhite slogans, set fire to buildings, turned over cars, smashed windows, and looted stores. Decades of pent-up frustrations were being unleashed in just a few nights.[6]

The rioters were angry. They had heard all about Lyndon Johnson's War on Poverty, part of the Great Society campaign. But that war wasn't helping them. In 1964, with his Great Society program slowly coming into being, Johnson's biggest struggle was with African-American leaders. They were becoming impatient after their years of peaceful political protest. Johnson thought his programs were actually beginning to make a difference.

If any difference was being made, a group of southern black people didn't see it. Led by civil rights activists James Forman and Robert Moses, this group formed the Mississippi Freedom Democratic party, an organization devoted to seating blacks among the Mississippi delegates to the Democratic National Convention later that year. This was no easy task. The white Democrats of Mississippi wanted no blacks in their delegation, and northern Democrats were not showing any clear opposition to this practice of excluding blacks, possibly because they did not want to bring any attention to the underrepresentation of blacks in their own delegations.

To Johnson the sudden appearance of militant and politically active blacks was troublesome. He felt he needed a decisive and peaceful election to carry out his programs in Congress. He didn't want the establishment to become frightened. Such civil rights leaders as Martin Luther King, Bayard Rustin, and Whitney Young agreed to a very weak "moratorium" against civil rights demonstrations that summer—at least until after the election in the fall.[7]

Johnson's own civil rights record was checkered. He was seen by the civil rights movement as a Southerner, but he was a new kind of Southerner. Although he had aligned himself with racial segregationists in his early congressional career, Johnson in 1957 led the fight for the Civil Rights Act and exhibited a lot of pro–civil rights tendencies as he took over for Kennedy. But he had never told anyone in any publicly recorded situation where he stood on the issue and no one could say for sure.

Did the young LBJ have any special compassion for his Mexican-American high school students in Pearsall? Did his refusal to sign the "Southern Manifesto" in 1956 show an unexpected understanding of the plight of blacks? (The Manifesto spoke out against U.S. Supreme Court decisions that seemed to grant increasing rights to African-Americans.)[8] In his history of the Kennedy-Johnson years, Walt Rostow states two possible explanations for Johnson's stand on the Southern Manifesto: Johnson, as a sensible man, began to see racial discrimination as a weak point of southern life. Or Johnson, as a "striving politician," saw no need to get involved in the Manifesto and all that went with it; he had more important issues to worry about.[9]

A third possibility, one not considered by Rostow but perhaps even more likely, was nose counting. Lyndon Johnson—founder of the White Stars back in college—was instinctively adept at studying the electorate and figuring out how to find unexpected voters. Johnson used black and Mexican-American voters to win a number of elections. These were voting blocs other politicians ignored. Johnson probably saw them as important in providing a margin of victory in a close election. In other words, he would rather use African-American voters than discriminate against them.

For all of his political ability, Johnson was unable to win the hearts of the growingly militant young civil rights advocates such as Stokely Carmichael, who would later marry South African folksinger Miriam Makeba and move to Africa. But LBJ had some clout with the older members of the movement, who could remember back to the Eisenhower administration. It had taken some courage for LBJ to back Eisenhower against the largely segregationist southern caucus in Congress.

But it would be difficult to hold back the demonstrators who were increasingly frustrated with the way civil rights was progressing in America. The early leaders of the civil rights movement came from the rural South, where farming, fishing, and hunting could keep a family alive in the face of unemployment. In the industrial North, a few weeks of unemployment could destroy a family, and poor African-American families were **112** in trouble.[10]

Blacks were rapidly leaving the rural parts of the nation and heading for the factories of Detroit, the skyscraper canyons of New York and Chicago, and the steel mills of Pittsburgh and Youngstown. Census figures show 2.7 million blacks living in urban areas in 1910 as opposed to 13.8 million in 1960. During the same period the black population in rural America declined from 7.1 to 5.1 million.

In planting his War on Poverty seeds in 1963, Johnson had exceeded the dreams of his own aides, and commanded them to expand the plan. Following a meeting at the Johnson Ranch in Texas, late in 1963 the administration earmarked $500 million to begin the War on Poverty. Another $500 million would be spread around the federal budget for such things as job training. Thus, the White House would be able to announce a $1 billion "war" effort, a considerable expenditure for the time, especially for a War on Poverty.[11]

In January of 1964, Johnson in his State of the Union address declared "unconditional war on poverty." The Great Society was under way. Within a year, Johnson would proudly look at a list of achievements that included Medicare—the nation's first health insurance for the poor—and a series of legislation-producing conferences that actually were dubbed "Great Society" meetings by the Johnson administration.

Eventually added to the list of new programs stemming from the Great Society was the Job Corps (designed to provide job training to minorities) and Operation Head Start (an attempt to give children in poorly funded school districts a taste of education on the theory that they would perform better once they started school). The Model Cities Program, created to clear away ghettos and build housing projects, was also begun during this period.

The programs would have a profound impact on the United States right up into the 1990s. The poverty rate for older Americans, for instance, was slashed from 28.5 percent in 1966 to 14.6 percent in 1982. But the budget deficits of the federal government were also growing cancerously. In 1984, Medicare, Medicaid, and food stamps cost taxpayers $115 billion. And the bureaucracy that was needed to support such ambitious programs grew unfathomably.[12]

Johnson should have been riding high at the time, but he faced increasing opposition. His opponents, including skeptical members of Congress like Eugene McCarthy and Americans for Democratic Action official Allard Lowenstein, insisted that Johnson was substituting programs for direct action.

Actually, the opposition may have had a point. It was Johnson's style to lavish federal money on all sorts of projects geared to win people over. That is how LBJ viewed the National Youth Agency under Roosevelt and that is how he continued to view the problems he faced in his own presidency. LBJ actually tried several approaches, but they all stemmed from the idea that federal funding would provide an answer to a serious problem.

Walt Rostow suggests that there were three separate approaches followed by LBJ in his efforts to break up the all-black inner-city neighborhoods that had come to be known as ghettos. (A ghetto is a section of a city whose inhabitants cannot come and go freely, as in the Warsaw Ghetto of World War II, in which Polish-Jewish inhabitants were imprisoned.)

The LBJ approaches included "functional programs" such as Operation Head Start, one of several projects aimed at stopping specific problems in the ghetto. Head Start gave basic education at the kindergarten level to preschool children and sought to reinforce their training as they entered the elementary grades.

Another approach was "development," a method of funding local projects in the same way the U.S. distributed foreign aid, the idea being that the poor sections of America could be enriched in much the same way as foreign countries became enriched through foreign aid. The disastrous Model Cities Program, created as a means to renew inner-city areas, became bogged down by corruption and mismanagement. Ironically, it *was* functioning a lot like foreign aid programs.

The final approach, in Rostow's view, was to stimulate the overall economy so that jobs would filter down to the inner cities and stimulate the economies of poor neighborhoods. That policy had worked during the Roosevelt administration.[13]

Still, although there was growing opposition from the unknown but emerging "new left," traditional liberals from the Roosevelt years and even some moderately conservative leaders seemed to embrace the Great Society idea. Martin Luther King, the liberal civil rights leader, and Henry Luce, the conservative publisher of *Time* and *Life* magazines, both endorsed the concept.[14]

King's support had a double edge. On the positive side, he influenced a large number of African-Americans. On the negative side, King—who was committed to nonviolent action against the evils of racism—was under increasing attack by militant younger blacks, who accused him of being too weak, and by conservative white leaders who regarded him as a threat and a leftist. King had befriended Johnson, however, and the black leader was on the record as opposed to communism. In his book, *The Strength to Love*, King said: "A true Christian cannot be a true Communist. . . ." This published doctrine left no doubt that King did not subscribe to Communist beliefs as some unfair enemies had charged. That left LBJ free to embrace King and his followers as political allies.[15]

The Great Society was the very essence of Democratic party politics of its day because it sought to harness the political power of the disfranchised, or outcast, groups like African-Americans, poor whites, and Native Americans. (Johnson was the first president to recognize Native American tribes as agencies to sponsor federally funded projects.)[16]

The Great Society was also created to help fight concerns about mounting economic problems. The Vietnam War, which Johnson had vowed to end with minimum loss of American lives, was growing larger day by day. Rising taxes and increasing unemployment had created a political pressure cooker.

LBJ himself felt strongly that he faced an uphill battle in convincing the American public that he had a right to govern. "Just being elected to the office does not guarantee him [the president] that right," Johnson noted. "Every president has to become a leader, and to be a leader he must attract people who are willing to follow him. Every president has to develop a moral underpinning of power or he soon discovers that he has no power at all."[17]

In her diary, Lady Bird wrote on January 23, 1964: "I really don't know how Lyndon can reach a moment of peace at the end of the day, but you couldn't have told it from his face. He looks relaxed, happy, successful, even after what must have been . . . a rather grueling press conference." That face would bear deep age lines within four years. The times were taking their toll on LBJ.[18]

Vietnam

If any issue carried Lyndon Baines Johnson into office in the biggest presidential landslide of American history to that date, it was the growing Vietnam War. In the 1964 election campaign Johnson focused on the "hawkish" stance Senator Barry Goldwater of Arizona had taken. Goldwater, a conservative Republican, had asserted that America should increase the Vietnam war effort quickly and decisively and should expect to win in Vietnam.

Johnson, with the help of a willing media, had turned Goldwater into a laughingstock, a would-be gunslinger from the faded Old West. At the height of the campaign, Johnson told one gathering: "We know how the West was won. It wasn't won by men on horses who tried to settle every argument with a quick draw and a shot from the hip."[1]

Johnson won the election with what was then a record 61 percent of the popular vote. He carried forty-four states. Voters increased the Democratic majority in both the House and Senate that year. Even in states where Republicans won new territory, these Republicans had liberal leanings. In Massachusetts, Republican attorney general Edward Brooke won the Senate seat despite Johnson's lopsided victory there. Brooke, a black man with some conservative ideas about business, was strongly opposed to Goldwater's Vietnam War ideas and was a liberal on racial issues. Republican governor George Romney of Michigan also swept to victory, despite Johnson's local landslide. Romney, too, was considered a liberal on most issues, at least by his fellow Republicans. Even Democrats saw him as a "moderate."[2]

Johnson had a better approach to Vietnam than Goldwater, LBJ's supporters argued. They couldn't be more specific except to say that LBJ could bring the combat to an end if given a little latitude. During the summer preceding the presidential election, Johnson used his powers of dealmaking and his newfound power as president to pressure Congress into giving him broad authority to continue the growing military action in Vietnam without actually declaring war. An undeclared war was not new in the American memory. The United States had entered the Korean "conflict" or "police action" without a congressional declaration of war.

Joseph Stalin, the strongman leader of the

Union of Soviet Socialist Republics, had devised a war in Korea less than twenty years earlier with the help of China's Communist party chairman, Mao Tse-tung. With Soviet and Chinese aid, North Korean soldiers invaded South Korea in 1950, and by 1951 the United States—as the main participant in a United Nations peacekeeping force—was defending a mass of land in South Korea below an imaginary line known as the 38th parallel. It was a bloody battle involving the "free world" versus the "communist world."[3]

Had Johnson launched into a war based on the Korean experience right away, Goldwater might have been able to defeat him. But Johnson needed an incident to help him increase the stakes in Vietnam—and one finally emerged.

The incident was really a series of firings on American Navy ships sitting in the Tonkin Gulf off the Vietnam coast. The attacks were allegedly unprovoked, although Johnson aides clearly knew the Vietnamese had first been attacked by an American-led force. Johnson himself may have knowingly misled Congress into passing the Tonkin Gulf Resolution, which allowed him to take "all necessary measures" to prevent future hostile fire against American naval vessels.[4]

The fighting, which had been ignored by most Americans for nearly a decade, was now growing in scope and importance. At first the area of fighting was called Indochina, a large thumb-shaped area of land with China as its dominant northeastern neighbor. A hodgepodge of tiny nations run by princes, Indochina included Vietnam, Laos, and Cambodia. These surrounded Thailand, once the proud kingdom of Siam, and the Malaysian peninsula. Americans had rarely given this land a thought since World War II.

In the years following World War II, vast changes took place throughout Asia, and Indochina was the boiling pot of intrigue. The French, who had colonized it, found Indochina to be too expensive to keep. Early in the 1950s, when the French Foreign Legion met with resounding defeat in battles with nationalist Vietnamese troops, the French withdrew and left a vacuum in Vietnam, Laos, and Cambodia. In these countries several factors were growing in importance. The three countries had been widely divided in terms of religious beliefs and cultural leanings, and the provinces had always been difficult to organize into a single unit.

Vietnam

For many politically aware Indochinese, nationalism naturally led to communism, since communism was dedicated to a singular central government. But which way to go within the Communist world? The Soviet Union was prepared to back military governments in all parts of Indochina, but so was the Chinese government in Peking—and the USSR and China did not get along.

The United States found itself becoming slowly entangled in these affairs during the Eisenhower administration, when the president began sending small numbers of military advisers to help anticommunist forces in Indochina, and especially in Vietnam. When President Kennedy took office in 1960, the situation remained bad, but was still not important to the American people.

It was Kennedy who decided to commit more advisers to Vietnam and to the increasingly powerful government of Ngo Dinh Diem, president of South Vietnam. In North Vietnam, Ho Chi Minh led a Communist government from the traditional national capital of Hanoi. In the south, Diem and his family took almost dictatorial control

121

and began to request increasing assistance from the United States.

By the time Lyndon Johnson became president in 1963, the media was referring to the events in Vietnam as a police action or impending war. Johnson felt a strong sense of commitment to resolve it as well as to protect American interests in Europe, where aggressive Soviet military movement was heightening pressures. Five days after Kennedy's death, Johnson vowed to Congress: "We will keep our commitments from South Vietnam to West Berlin."

The American public had already invested—and come out ahead—in Europe. World War II had been a war against totalitarian oppression across Europe, and Americans looked back at the war as one the United States had won. Americans were fairly united in their desire to keep the Soviets from taking away any ground won in that war, so Johnson's reference to West Berlin was well received. But Vietnam was another story. Johnson asserted that he really didn't know the details of what was going on there until forty-eight hours after taking office. "Ambassador Henry Cabot Lodge . . . was optimistic. He believed the recent change of government in Saigon was an improvement." That new government had overthrown Ngo Dinh Diem and had assassinated him just two weeks before the Kennedy assassination. The new South Vietnamese government was under the rulership of a group of generals. Johnson believed their leadership would not be corrupt, as Diem's most certainly had been.[5]

Despite his protestations of ignorance about the growing problems in Vietnam, LBJ must have known more than he claims because as vice president he had gone to Vietnam as Kennedy's representative.

The realities of the growing Vietnam War were also closing in on Johnson in 1964. Johnson knew, in his own words,

> History provided too many cases where the sound of the bugle put an immediate end to the hopes and dreams of the best reformers; the Spanish-American War drowned the Populist spirit; World War I ended Woodrow Wilson's New Freedom. . . . Yet everything I knew about history told me that if I got out of Vietnam and let [North Vietnamese leader] Ho Chi Minh run through the streets of Saigon . . . I'd be giving a big fat reward to aggression.[6]

As with most of his life, LBJ gave many different accounts of how he felt at that moment. He once insisted that he was skeptical from the start about the new government and about American involvement in Vietnam. But the fact remains that any skepticism he claims to have had was belied by the events that unfolded under his leadership. Vietnam underscored LBJ's greatest weakness: he was not an executive, he was a deal-maker.

After defeating Goldwater in 1964, and with the Tonkin Gulf Resolution in hand, Johnson set to work on Vietnam in 1965. A little more than 200 Americans had died there by the time Johnson was elected. By the time he left office, the U.S. military presence had risen to over half a million and American casualties had grown into the tens of thousands.[7]

What was America doing in Vietnam? Clearly, Johnson had rejected the Goldwater position that America should exert all its power to finish the war quickly. Johnson had no stomach for such an over-

Lyndon

Baines

Johnson

whelming display of power against such a small foe. Yet Johnson was no "dove" himself. He felt that the Truman Doctrine, invoked by President Harry S Truman in the 1940s, gave the United States the right to settle the Vietnam conflict.

As LBJ's secretary of state, Dean Rusk, put it, the doctrine stated that "We can be safe only to the extent that our total environment is safe." By "total environment," Rusk referred to the entire free world and any country that cared to join it. Outside that world was international communism, which most Americans considered to be in opposition to freedom.

The Truman Doctrine had been invoked to prevent sudden military takeovers in Greece and Turkey right after World War II. Truman had asserted that America had the right to send troops into a foreign country whose freedom was under siege. The ultimate goal was to contain communism, that is, to keep it from spreading. But whereas some European allies supported Truman's position in Europe, no country was willing to back the U.S. policy in Vietnam—not even France, which had fled.[8]

And as Johnson took office, a "loyal opposition" in Congress was rising against the Vietnam effort. It is not a little ironic that Johnson himself refers back to his days in the halls of Congress when describing the way he felt about the growing division in America over Vietnam:

> I could not forget the refusal of the House of Representatives in 1939 and 1940 to provide $5 million in funds for the strengthening of Guam, for fear of antagonizing the Japanese. I could not forget the long and difficult fight over the Selective Service [military draft] Act

in 1940, when major wars were already being fought in both Europe and China.

As a legislator, Johnson had often compromised his own goals and coaxed others to do the same with theirs. As president he could not understand why he couldn't continue doing that.[9]

What Americans wanted to know more than anything else was, Why are we in Vietnam? In February of 1966 the chairman of the Joint Chiefs of Staff, General Maxwell Taylor, was asked the big question on NBC's "Meet the Press." He answered by defining U.S. goals in terms of a projected victory in Vietnam: "Victory is just accomplishing what we set out to do, to allow South Vietnam to choose its own government and have Hanoi cease the aggression. That's victory." Less than two years later, the new chairman of the Joint Chiefs, General William Westmoreland, acknowledged that the Vietnamese enemies could never be defeated "in a traditional or classic sense."[10]

By 1967, millions of Americans considered themselves "antiwar" and the antiwar movement was extremely powerful politically. Just a few years earlier, the movement had been composed largely of left-wing extremists and young people who felt left out of the process that threatened to send them to war. But it had now grown to include major figures from the political establishment as well as Martin Luther King, Jr., himself, whose presence gave the movement strength and legitimacy in the eyes of blacks and liberal whites.[11]

Ordinary citizens who had never participated in politics before were now circulating petitions against the war. Pioneering rock music "festivals" to raise money for opposition to the war were becoming almost common. In the winter of 1969 **125** thousands of music lovers gathered in New York's Madison Square Garden to join singers Peter, Paul, and Mary; Harry Belafonte; Jimi Hendrix; Judy Collins; Richie Havens; and others in speaking out against the war. The brothers Daniel and Philip Berrigan, both Jesuit priests, poured blood on certain federal documents and set fire to others in protest.[12]

Civil rights frustration, economic problems, and other stumbling blocks were standing in the way of Johnson's reelection in 1968—but the Vietnam War is probably the one issue that brought him down. It was the issue around which a speechwriter for Vice President Hubert Humphrey, Allard K. Lowenstein, created the Dump Johnson movement in 1967.[13]

LBJ
Bows Out

On March 31, 1968, Lyndon Baines Johnson stunned the American public with a disclosure that only his closest family members expected. He was not going to stand for reelection; he was not going to take on Eugene McCarthy, a fellow Democrat, or Richard Nixon, his Republican rival. Instead, Johnson was going to bow off the great stage of public life. And, in so doing, he hoped that a treaty ending the Vietnam War could be drawn up.

It was a shock because Johnson was not doing all that badly in the polls. It was a shock because he had not really accomplished the goals set forth at the start of his presidency. To those who were closest to him it would have been less of a shock. The Johnson family had a history of heart attack and stroke, and LBJ himself had suffered a heart attack in 1955. In his own account of his presidency, LBJ said: "Whenever I walked through the Red Room [of the White House] and saw the portrait of [former president] Woodrow Wilson hanging there I thought of him stretched out upstairs in the White House, powerless to move, with the machinery of the American government in disarray around him."[1]

By April 3 Johnson's hopes that he might have some part in ending the Vietnam War were revived. The North Vietnamese government had announced its willingness to come to the peace table in Washington. Johnson was right, and he luxuriated in that rightness. But the next day, Martin Luther King, Jr., was shot to death in cold blood by a racist drifter named James Earl Ray while King was touring Tennessee and making appearances for striking sanitation workers. In Johnson's words: ". . . it became immediately clear that his assassination had compounded the danger of violence." There would be rioting in the streets.[2]

Clearly Lyndon Johnson's world was closing in on him. The Vietnam War appeared to be going on forever. And the "guns and butter" promises of the Great Society seemed to be losing credibility. "Guns and butter," or the theory that the economy could support both the war in Vietnam and the war on poverty, was Johnson's own answer to critics who attacked him for spending millions of dollars a day on the Vietnam War, and far less on federal poverty programs. Critics said the war was bleeding the domestic programs of cash. And the domestic programs were bleeding taxpayers.

Model Cities, Johnson's plan to rebuild urban America, ran into serious fiscal and political problems early on. Critics referred to urban renewal programs under the Model Cities as "urban removal," meaning the federal projects succeeded only in leveling buildings and destroying old neighborhoods. There were critics on every side—especially in the media.

As with other American presidents, Johnson found the scrutiny of newspapers, magazines, radio, television, and even political polltakers to be at times unbearable. In his book *The Ultimate Tyranny*, former senator Eugene McCarthy quotes Johnson as telling newly elected vice president Spiro Agnew in 1968: "Young man, we have in this country two big television networks, NBC and CBS. We have two news magazines, *Newsweek* and *Time*. We have two wire services, AP and UPI. We have two pollsters, Gallup and Harris. We have two big newspapers, *The Washington Post* and the *New York Times*. They're all so damned big they think they own the country. But, young man, don't get any ideas about fighting."

Such was Lyndon Johnson's view of the world watching him in the year of his great defeat. He often sat in the Oval Office of the White House watching three television screens at once. Next to these he had two wire-service teletypewriters that carried the news from AP and UPI, the same news that newspapers and the broadcast media received.

He had become so careful, some would even say paranoid, about what was said about him and around him that he began to extend his love for gadgets to a new love for electronic bugging devices. The White House was wired for sound almost everywhere, and it would have been difficult for anyone to know whether they were being tape-recorded by the president on any given day.

Investigative columnist Jack Anderson would later write in *Popular Mechanics* magazine that Johnson taped every conversation in the Oval Office. He tells a story of a visit to the Oval Office by Robert Kennedy a year before Kennedy's death. Kennedy carried a briefcase and sat down near a fireplace where the president had directed him. They chatted for quite some time, and when they were finished, Kennedy rose, shook LBJ's hand, and left. When he returned to his own office, Anderson wrote, Kennedy played back the tape. It was blank. It had been jammed by an electronic device in LBJ's office.[3]

The Vietnam War and rioting in the streets had taken their toll, and in 1967 there emerged a "Dump Johnson" campaign run by young liberals and supported by Johnson's old nemesis, Allard Lowenstein and the ADA. At the beginning of 1967 there were over 400,000 troops in Vietnam. The war had cost about $22 billion the previous year, when the Johnson administration spent only $1.2 billion on the War on Poverty.[4]

Cruel parodies of Johnson's person and his style were found everywhere. In New York's Greenwicc Village a musical comedy titled *MacBird* showed the president as a country bumpkin with his hand in every cash register. Walt Kelley, the cartoonist whose character Pogo had delighted a national readership and vexed politicians for half a century, depicted LBJ as a character called The Lone Arranger. This characterization painted Johnson as a foolish politician who worked so hard appeasing everyone that he appeased no one. In some episodes the Lone Arranger was shown making deals with a character who looked vaguely like

Mao Tse Tung, then dictator of the communist People's Republic of China.

He seemed to be in a no-win situation. On television he came off as a clumsy and often belligerent person with no warmth and little character. As journalist Milton Viorst noted, Johnson was meant to "persuade nose to nose in a back room of the Senate, not to address a hundred million people on a television screen." Indeed, his entire life had been spent "working the system." His wangling power at San Marcos, his moves on the rooms of power in Congress, his working the Senate cloakroom—all this had built up credentials the American public did not see as presidential. Johnson had what was commonly called "a credibility gap."

It hit him hardest in Congress, where powerful members felt that Johnson had let them down in a variety of political and personal ways. The war situation was not improving, and LBJ was taking more and more exclusive credit for the Great Society programs, which he could not have built without the help of Congress. To make matters worse, the never-ending war was beginning to cost so much money that Johnson had to exact more revenues, and that meant more taxes.

This would be the final straw with his friends in Congress. He had talked a lot in previous years about "guns and butter," about an American economy that was so strong it could accomplish anything. But now it was clear that some spending cuts would have to be made and some new taxes collected to pay for the war. The result was a 6 percent income tax surcharge. House Ways and Means Committee chairman Wilbur Mills was willing to back the surcharge only after LBJ agreed to go on TV and let his Vietnam War policy take the responsibility for both the tax increase and the impending cut in funds for Great Society programs.[5]

Johnson was losing influence, but his family remained loyal and he never ran out of friends. In his final writings about his own presidency, Johnson said: "It has been said that the Presidency is the loneliest office in the world. I did not find it so. Even during the darkest hours of my administration, I always knew that I could draw on the strength, support, and love of my family and friends."

But LBJ had clearly aged during the brief years of his presidency and it had clearly taken an emotional toll on both him and his family. He had enjoyed much company during those years. But, he acknowledged, ". . . if I was seldom lonely, I was often alone. No one can exerience with the President of the United States the glory and agony of his office. No one can share his majestic view from his pinnacle of power. No one can share the burden of his decisions or the scope of his duties."[6]

Over LBJ's four years in office, Lady Bird had expressed the frequent hope that he would leave office after his first full term. This was not a decision to be taken lightly. Johnson often paced the floor of the Oval Office contemplating how he would, how he could, do it.

Always the family man, he brought the issue before Luci and Lynda as well as Lady Bird. "Luci did not want me to run," he recalled. "She insisted that she wanted a living father. Lynda's response was more complex. As a daughter, she said, she preferred that I not run, but as a citizen she hoped I would. Later, when her husband Marine Capt. Charles Robb [who would later become governor of and then a senator of Virginia] was under orders to go to Vietnam, her reaction as a citizen superseded her reaction as a daughter."[7]

The family greeted LBJ's decision with mixed joy and sorrow, as would be expected of those about to give up a position of power and glamour but who wanted to see their father and husband survive. Clearly, Johnson and his family expected his resignation to place him in a positive light as a great statesman who placed the desire for peace in Vietnam above his political ambitions. But in the months that followed this seemed a futile hope. The assassination of Martin Luther King, Jr., precipitated weeks of rioting across the country and gave birth to a new sense of fear about the future. And while the nation was still recovering from the shock of King's killing in June, tragedy struck again.

Robert Kennedy had entered the presidential race and was now giving front-runner Eugene McCarthy quite a run for the Democratic nomination. In the California primary the two ran so close that newspapers across the country had to reprint almost every hour as the lead between the two changed. On the evening of June 5, as he was about to take the California primary and place a serious roadblock in McCarthy's march to the presidency, Robert F. Kennedy was assassinated in a Los Angeles hotel by a gun-toting Sirhan B. Sirhan. The nation was in mourning for days.[8]

While LBJ mourned publicly, biographer Doris Kearns notes that the president later said of RFK:

> It would have been hard on me to watch Bobby march to "Hail to the Chief," but I almost wish he had become president so the country could finally see a flesh and blood Kennedy grap-

pling with the daily work of the presidency and all the inevitable disappointments instead of their storybook image of great heroes who, because they were dead, could make anything anyone wanted happen.[9]

Clearly, Johnson was bitter about RFK's public image in death as well as in life.

The presidential nominating conventions that followed were frightening dramatizations that ran completely out of control. Demonstrators against the Vietnam War and for improved conditions for African-American and other minority communities tried to shut the convention down in July of 1968. Against this background, the Republican party nominated Richard Nixon as its presidential standard-bearer. Meanwhile, in Chicago later that summer, the Democrats held a frequently disrupted convention that saw the arrests of hundreds of young demonstrators, who were sometimes beaten by stick-carrying police before a horrified national TV news audience.

Hubert Humphrey won the Democratic nomination, but by summer's end it was clear that the Democrats were politically bankrupt and that Johnson was leaving what might be called a rapidly sinking ship. With just a couple of months to go in the White House, LBJ struck the pose of a tired and aging man. He was widely viewed as a loser in much the same way as some of his neighbors once viewed his father. There were few friends cheering him on as his presidency came to a close.[10]

LBJ's
Last Days

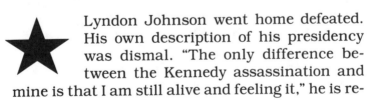 Lyndon Johnson went home defeated. His own description of his presidency was dismal. "The only difference between the Kennedy assassination and mine is that I am still alive and feeling it," he is reported to have said.[1]

He had fallen from a landslide victory against Barry Goldwater in 1964 to a point at which he wasn't even assured of his party's renomination in 1968, four very short years. His vast creative energy and willingness to compromise everything had led him into the loftiest courts of power through the most obscure entrances. But it was not the sort of career most people admire. If anyone ever made much out of little, it was Lyndon Johnson, a man who could launch himself all the way to the White House from the initial lowly position of running errands in Congress.

LBJ was a man given to exaggeration. By the time of his retirement to the Johnson Ranch, LBJ's initials were synonymous with the "credibility gap," the sense the American media and public had that their leaders were not forthright. Of his own assessment of his presidency, LBJ warned readers: "I make no pretense of having written a complete and definitive history of my Presidency. . . . I have not written these chapters to say, 'This is how it was,' but to say, 'This is how I saw it from my vantage point.'" This was very defensive language from a man who longed for historical credibility.[2]

And surely time was to provide him with some of that credibility. His Medicare program, despite its many administrative and funding problems, remained a vital part of government services twenty years after Johnson's death. His Glassboro (New Jersey) State College meeting with Soviet leader Aleksei Kosygin in June of 1967 was a landmark in the history of the Cold War. Finally, the United States was seeking help from the Soviet Union in striking a peace agreement with Vietnam. It was a diplomatic coup, even if it didn't work. He handled the transition from the Kennedy administration admirably.

But his greatest triumphs were in the civil rights field. A skeptic could well imagine that LBJ used the issue to gain votes from the growing new constituency of African-Americans. That was certainly on his mind. But there was also a righteous side to Lyndon Johnson. He introduced bills that

John Kennedy had refused to consider because JFK didn't believe they would pass Congress.

Former ambassador and now syndicated newspaper columnist Carl T. Rowan was one of the closest to Johnson when it came to civil rights. Rowan recalls:

> Lyndon Baines Johnson was egocentric, domineering, imperious, mean, insecure, cornpone, unfaithful, crude. He was also generous, brave, a fighter for the little guy, loyal to friends and causes—and damned effective. It all depended on which LBJ you encountered, with how much Cutty Sark [whiskey] in him, or how many woes and worries were beating down upon him.

Rowan says that when all the facts are added up, Johnson was "the greatest human rights and civil rights president America has ever known."

In a 1964 speech introducing civil rights legislation, President Johnson tried to take all the emotion out of the civil rights debate and reduce the discourse to an honest assessment of how America had to change. LBJ said:

> There is no constitutional issue here. The command of the Constitution is plain. There is no moral issue. It is wrong to deny any of your fellow Americans the right to vote. . . . There is no issue of states' rights, or national rights. There is only the struggle for human rights. . . .[3]

In the end, the man who tried so hard to be different from his father, to be practical rather than idealistic, bailed out of the White House proclaiming: "Now my service was over, and it had ended without my having had to haul down the flag, compromise my principles or run out on my obligations." Unlike his father, he did manage to consult with his family before making the move, but he seemed unable to escape his own history.

Most of his biographers say Lyndon Johnson's life was practically ended on the day he left Washington in January of 1969. His health, which had been declining, continued to decline until his death. In the end, Lyndon Johnson felt frustrated that he could not adequately convey to the American public what he had gone through in his presidency. It reminded him of his own father saying to him, "Son, you will never understand what it is to be a father until you are a father."[4]

LBJ spent the last day of his presidency with members of his Cabinet. He had a final lunch at the home of the secretary of defense Clark Clifford and his wife, Mary, in Bethesda, Maryland. Dean Rusk, who as secretary of state had tried to help Johnson shore up a crumbling Vietnam war effort, also attended, as did Ambassador Averell Harriman and others. Johnson presented Medals of Freedom to five of the attendees; then he and Lady Bird boarded *Air Force One* for their last presidential flight: the return trip to Texas.

On arriving home in Austin, Johnson was met by a crowd. He told them:

> Let us try to help our new leader, who after all is the only President we have. I hope that you will be as good to him as you have been to me, understanding in time of crisis, strong in supporting when we needed you. . . . We left a lot of unsolved problems on Mr. Nixon's desk not because we wanted to but because the times in which we lived required us to.

Again, he was defensive in his homecoming speech. He used the words of a jilted lover: "I hope that you will be as good to him as you have been to me." He excused himself for leaving problems on the desk of his replacement.[5]

He then went home to the LBJ Ranch, where he would soon engage in a struggle with heart disease that would lead to his death. LBJ would probably have been content to raise cattle on the ranch, write a three-volume memoir (he finished only the first volume), and establish his presidential library. But by the spring of 1970 he was in Brooke Army Hospital in San Antonio suffering from chest pains. The diagnosis was angina, a disease generally connected with hardened arteries. Biographer and friend Doris Kearns said Johnson's strength was slipping.[6]

Indeed, he was not sleeping well in his last year of life, a year in which Kearns often slept at the Johnson ranch. She recalls his waking her up at five-thirty in the morning, wanting to talk about his childhood.

On the afternoon of January 22, 1973, two days after Richard Nixon took the presidential oath of office for a second time, Lyndon Baines Johnson retired to his room for a nap. He had been suffering from frequent attacks of angina. He was sixty-four years old, but by most accounts and many news photos he seemed much older.

He napped in a sunny room not far from the place of his birth along the Pedernales. Now things were different. He had accomplished much in his life. He had become, as he had vowed he would, president of the United States. He and Lady Bird had built a strong business of their radio and TV holdings. The ranch was in excellent condition, the best it had ever been, and the LBJ Library on the campus of the University of Texas at Austin was about to become one of the most visited presidential libraries in America.

Still, he had lived the past four years out of the limelight and out of the action, and he had never won the recognition he felt he deserved. So it was probably with a certain amount of bitterness and sadness that LBJ dozed off. At about four in the afternoon, he telephoned his Secret Service escorts, who were on the ranch, that he was ill and needed help. By the time help arrived, the former president was dead. Lady Bird had gone off for the afternoon and was not with him in his final moments.[7]

President Nixon said of LBJ, "No man had greater dreams for America." In his *New York Times* column of January 23, journalist Max Frankel said LBJ went to his grave expecting history to vindicate him. Perhaps, Frankel said, after the Vietnam War was long over and racial strife was just a memory, historians would look back kindly on LBJ and pronounce him one of the leaders who made America a great place to live for everyone. But even Frankel, who seemed to agree with LBJ, had to acknowledge that it would take a long time.[8]

LBJ was buried a few days later in the family plot at the LBJ Ranch, on the northern bank of the Pedernales next to the graves of his mother and father. Former Texas governor John Connally and the evangelist Billy Graham spoke final words of comfort to the family. Mrs. Johnson remained at the ranch, where she continued running family businesses, the library, and a highly successful new project aimed at preserving wildflowers across America. As of this writing she continues to work on the wildflowers project. Historians have yet to give LBJ the credit he supposedly expected, but the wounds of Vietnam and the issues surrounding civil rights continue to plague the nation. If Max Frankel was right, then the LBJ legacy may not be complete for many years to come.

LBJ's Last

Days

Source Notes

Chapter 1

1. Merle Miller, *Lyndon, An Oral Biography* (New York: Putnam, 1980), p. 3.
2. *New York Times,* August 22, 1908, p. 16.
3. Ibid.
4. Ibid., August 24, 1908, p. 3.
5. Robert A. Caro, *The Years of Lyndon Johnson—The Path to Power* (New York: Knopf, 1982), p. 5.
6. Ibid., p. 21.
7. Rose Houk, *Heart's Home—Lyndon B. Johnson's Hill Country* (Austin, Tex.: Southwest Parks and Monuments Association, 1986), p. 4.
8. Miller, p. 6.
9. Ibid., p. 15.
10. Sam Houston Johnson, *My Brother Lyndon* (New York: Cowles Book Company, 1970), p. 6.
11. Ibid., pp. 10–11.
12. Clarke Newlon, *L.B.J. The Man From Johnson City* (New York: Dodd, Mead, 1976), p. 25.
13. Ibid., p. 28.
14. Ronnie Dugger, *The Politician—The Life and Times of Lyndon Johnson* (New York: Norton, 1982), p. 90.
15. Newlon, p. 29.
16. Miller, p. 23.
17. Caro, pp. 121–122.
18. Ibid.
19. Ibid., pp. 122–123.

Chapter 2

1. Robert Dallek, *Lone Star Rising* (New York: Oxford University Press, 1991), pp. 26–30.
2. Clarke Newlon, *L.B.J.: The Man From Johnson City* (New York: Dodd, Mead, 1976), p. 30.
3. Ronnie Dugger, *The Politician—The Life and Times of Lyndon Johnson* (New York: Norton, 1982), p. 95.
4. Ibid., p. 108.
5. Ibid., p. 100.
6. Sam Houston Johnson, *My Brother Lyndon* (New York: Cowles Book Company, 1970), pp. 23–24.
7. Dugger, p. 109.
8. Doris Kearns, *Lyndon Johnson and the American Dream* (New York: Harper & Row, 1976), p. 48.
9. Sam Houston Johnson, pp. 26–29.
10. Merle Miller, *An Oral Biography* (New York: Putnam, 1980), p. 29.
11. Ibid., p. 30.
12. Robert A. Caro, *The Years of Lyndon Johnson—The Path to Power* (New York: Vintage Books, 1983), p. 178.
13. Ibid.
14. Ibid., p. 179.
15. Miller, p. 30.

Chapter 3

1. Robert A. Caro, *The Years of Lyndon Johnson—The Path to Power* (New York: Vintage Books, 1983), p. 112.
2. Merle Miller, *Lyndon, An Oral Biography* (New York: Putnam, 1980), p. 24.
3. Caro, p. 113.
4. Ibid.
5. Doris Kearns, *Lyndon Johnson and the American Dream* (New York: Harper & Row, 1976), p. 56.
6. Caro, pp. 161–163.

7. Ronnie Dugger, *The Politician—The Life and Times of Lyndon Johnson* (New York: Norton, 1982), p. 124.
8. Caro, p. 163.
9. Ibid., pp. 163, 172–173.
10. Robert Dallek, *Lone Star Rising* (New York: Oxford University Press, 1991), pp. 113–115.
11. Ibid.
12. Caro, p. 300.
13. Miller, p. 44.
14. Sam Houston Johnson, *My Brother Lyndon* (New York: Cowles Book Company, 1970), p. 40.
15. Ibid., p. 41.
16. Miller, pp. 44–46.
17. Alfred Steinberg, *Sam Johnson's Boy* (New York: Macmillan, 1968), p. 89.
18. Dallek, pp. 114–115.

Chapter 4

1. Robert A. Caro, *The Years of Lyndon Johnson—The Path to Power* (New York: Vintage Books, 1983), p. 205.
2. Ibid., pp. 202–204.
3. Alfred Steinberg, *Sam Johnson's Boy* (New York: Macmillan, 1968), pp. 61–66.
4. Caro, pp. 207–210.
5. Merle Miller, *Lyndon, An Oral Biography* (New York: Putnam, 1980), p. xvi.
6. Ronnie Dugger, *The Politician—The Life and Times of Lyndon Johnson* (New York: Norton, 1982), pp. 166–168.
7. Ibid., p. 165.
8. Ibid., pp. 172–173.
9. Ibid., p. 175.
10. Doris Kearns, *Lyndon Johnson and the American Dream* (New York: Harper & Row, 1976), pp. 84–85.
11. *New York Times*, April 11, 1937, p. 1.

12. Steinberg, p. 97.
13. Robert Caro, "Annals of Politics—The Johnson Years: A Congressman Goes to War," *New Yorker*, November 6, 1989, p. 93.

Chapter 5

1. Merle Miller, *Lyndon, An Oral Biography* (New York: Putnam, 1980), p. 79.
2. Ibid., p. 78.
3. Robert Caro, *The Years of Lyndon Johnson—The Path to Power* (New York: Vintage Books, 1983) pp. 739–740.
4. John Bartlett, *Familiar Quotations* (Boston: Little, Brown, 1980), p. 780.
5. Caro, "Annals of Politics—The Johnson Years: A Congressman Goes to War," *New Yorker*, November 6, 1989, p. 94.
6. Miller, p. 98.
7. Doris Kearns, *Lyndon Johnson and the American Dream* (New York: Harper & Row, 1976), p. 93.
8. Alfred Steinberg, *Sam Johnson's Boy* (New York: Macmillan, 1968), pp. 244–246.
9. Kearns, p. 101.
10. Sam Houston Johnson, *My Brother Lyndon* (New York: Cowles Book Company, 1970), p. 77.
11. Larry L. King, "My Hero LBJ," *Harper's* magazine, October 1966, p. 53.
12. Sam Houston Johnson, pp. 82–83.
13. Ibid., pp. 84–86.
14. Robert Dallek, *Lone Star Rising* (New York: Oxford University Press, 1991), pp. 166–167.
15. W. W. Rostow, *The Diffusion of Power* (New York: Macmillan, 1972), p. 303.
16. George Reedy, "The True Dawn of Civil Rights," *Washington Monthly,* May 1982, pp. 46–51.
17. Carl T. Rowan, "Breaking Barriers: A Memoire" (book review), *Ebony*, December 1990, p. 76.
18. Author's interview with Lynda Johnson Robb. (A

transcript of the interview has been turned over to the LBJ Library in Austin.)

Chapter 6

1. Doris Kearns, *Lyndon Johnson and the American Dream* (New York: Harper & Row, 1976), pp. 160–162.
2. Arthur M. Schlesinger, Jr., *Robert Kennedy and His Times* (Boston: Houghton Mifflin, 1978), p. 206.
3. Ralph de Toledano, *R.F.K., The Man Who Would Be President* (New York: Putnam, 1967), p. 141.
4. Ibid., p. 157.
5. Milton Viorst, *Fire in the Streets* (New York: Simon and Schuster, 1979), p. 238.
6. Ralph de Toledano, "If It's Goldwater v. Johnson, Who Will Win?" *National Review*, 1964, pp. 101–102.
7. Kearns, p. 161.
8. Paul K. Conkin, *Big Daddy from the Pedernales* (Boston: Twayne Publishers, 1986), p. 153.
9. Sam Houston Johnson, *My Brother Lyndon* (New York: Cowles Book Company, 1970), pp. 106–108.
10. Walter Bennet, "Politics: The Coming Battle," *Time*, July 25, 1960, pp. 8–16.
11. Merle Miller, *Lyndon, An Oral Biography* (New York: Putnam, 1980), pp. 263–265.
12. Ibid., p. 262.

Chapter 7

1. John Bartlett, *Familiar Quotations* (Boston: Little, Brown, 1980), p. 381.
2. Ralph de Toledano, *R.F.K., The Man Who Would Be President* (New York: Putnam, 1967), p. 210.
3. W. W. Rostow, *The Diffusion of Power* (New York: Macmillan, 1972), pp. 304–305.
4. Paul K. Conkin, *Big Daddy from the Pedernales* (Boston: Twayne Publishers, 1986), pp. 143–145.

5. Sam Houston Johnson, *My Brother Lyndon* (New York: Cowles Book Company, 1970), p. 109.

6. Lyndon Baines Johnson, *The Vantage Point* (New York: Holt, Rinehart and Winston, 1971), pp. 52–54.

7. Rostow, p. 305.

8. Norman Ritter, "Battle of the Farm," *Life,* September 26, 1960, p. 92.

9. Alfred Steinberg, *Sam Johnson's Boy* (New York: Macmillan, 1968), p. 561.

10. Ibid., pp. 561–562.

11. Conkin, pp. 162–163.

12. Ibid.

Chapter 8

1. Lyndon Baines Johnson, *The Vantage Point* (New York: Holt, Rinehart and Winston, 1971), p. 1.

2. Ibid., p. 5.

3. Lady Bird Johnson, *A White House Diary* (New York: Holt, Rinehart and Winston, 1970), p. 4.

4. Lyndon Baines Johnson, p. 26.

5. Ibid., pp. 26–27.

6. Robert J. Donovan, *A Concise Compendium of the Warren Commission Report on the Assassination of John F. Kennedy* (New York: Popular Library, 1964), p. 17.

7. Lyndon Baines Johnson, p. 15.

8. W. W. Rostow, *The Diffusion of Power* (New York: Macmillan, 1972), p. 149.

9. J. B. West, *Upstairs at the White House* (New York: Coward, McCann and Geoghegan, 1973), p. 276.

10. Rostow, pp. 305–306.

11. Traphes Bryant, with Frances Spatz Leighton, *Dog Days at the White House* (New York: Macmillan, 1975), p. 97.

12. Lady Bird Johnson, p. vii.

13. Ibid., p. 74.

Lyndon

Baines

Johnson

14. Sam Houston Johnson, *My Brother Lyndon* (New York: Cowles Book Company, 1970), p. 112.
15. Author's interview with Lynda Johnson Robb.
16. Lady Bird Johnson, p. 13.
17. Lyndon Baines Johnson, pp. 20–21.

Chapter 9

1. Lyndon Baines Johnson, *The Vantage Point* (New York: Holt, Rinehart and Winston, 1971), p. 71.
2. Doris Kearns, *Lyndon Johnson and the American Dream* (New York: Harper & Row, 1976), p. 202.
3. Eugene McCarthy, *The Ultimate Tyranny* (New York: Harcourt Brace Jovanovich, 1980), p. 191.
4. Lyndon Baines Johnson, p. 28.
5. "Sit-ins' Successful Strategy," *Life,* September 19, 1960, p. 40.
6. Milton Viorst, *Fire in the Streets* (New York: Simon and Schuster, 1979), p. 311.
7. Ibid., p. 256.
8. W. W. Rostow, *The Diffusion of Power* (New York: Macmillan, 1972), p. 337.
9. Ibid., pp. 337–338.
10. Ibid., p. 341.
11. Lyndon Baines Johnson, p. 74.
12. Gordon Witkin, "Great Society: How Great Has It Been?" *U.S. News & World Report,* July 2, 1984, p. 31.
13. Rostow, pp. 343–346.
14. Kearns, p. 212.
15. Martin Luther King, Jr., *Strength to Love* (Philadelphia: Fortress Press, 1963), p. 96.
16. Vine Deloria, Jr., and Clifton Lytle, *The Nations Within* (New York: Pantheon, 1984), p. 184.
17. Lyndon Baines Johnson, p. 18.
18. Lady Bird Johnson, *A White House Diary* (New York: Holt, Rinehart and Winston, 1970), p. 59.

Chapter 10

1. Ronnie Dugger, *The Politician—The Life and Times of Lyndon Johnson* (New York: Norton, 1982), p. 131.
2. "The Elections: Year of the Democrat," *Newsweek*, November 16, 1964, p. 35.
3. W. W. Rostow, *The Diffusion of Power* (New York: Macmillan, 1972), pp. 12–14.
4. Vaughn Davis Bornet, *The Presidency of Lyndon B. Johnson* (Lawrence: University Press of Kansas, 1983), pp. 79–80.
5. Lyndon Baines Johnson, *The Vantage Point* (New York: Holt, Rinehart and Winston, 1971), p. 43.
6. Doris Kearns, *Lyndon Johnson and the American Dream* (New York: Harper & Row, 1976), pp. 252–253.
7. Bornet, p. 268.
8. Robert W. Tucker, "Their Wars, Our Choices," *New Republic*, October 24, 1983, pp. 22–23.
9. Lyndon Baines Johnson, p. 46.
10. Bornet, p. 262.
11. Milton Viorst, *Fire in the Streets* (New York: Simon and Schuster, 1979), p. 405.
12. Bornet, p. 256.
13. Viorst, p. 409.

Chapter 11

1. Lyndon Baines Johnson, *The Vantage Point* (New York: Holt, Rinehart and Winston, 1971), p. 425.
2. Ibid., p. 538.
3. Jack Anderson, "The Bugging of the White House," *Popular Mechanics*, July 1982, p. 64.
4. Milton Viorst, *Fire in the Streets* (New York: Simon and Schuster, 1979), p. 383.
5. Doris Kearns, *Lyndon Johnson and the American Dream* (New York: Harper & Row, 1976), p. 300.

Lyndon

Baines

Johnson

6. Lyndon Baines Johnson, p. ix (preface).
7. Ibid., p. 427.
8. Vaughn Davis Bornet, *The Presidency of Lyndon B. Johnson* (Lawrence: University Press of Kansas, 1983), pp. 307–309.
9. Kearns, p. 350.
10. Ibid., pp. 310–313.

Chapter 12
1. Larry L. King, "Machismo in the White House," *American Heritage*, vol. 27(5), 1976, p. 98.
2. Lyndon Baines Johnson, *The Vantage Point* (New York: Holt, Rinehart and Winston, 1971), p. ix (preface).
3. Carl T. Rowan, "Was LBJ the Greatest Civil Rights President Ever?" *Ebony*, December 1990, p. 76.
4. Lyndon Baines Johnson, p. 567.
5. Ibid., p. 568.
6. Doris Kearns, *Lyndon Johnson and the American Dream* (New York: Harper & Row, 1976), p. 15.
7. Ibid., p. 366.
8. *New York Times*, January 23, 1973, p. 1.

Bibliography

The notes below serve to help the reader locate sources that for various reasons would be particularly good reading. Each comment should give the reader an idea of why that particular book might be useful.

Bornet, Vaughn Davis. *The Presidency of Lyndon B. Johnson.* Lawrence: University Press of Kansas, 1983. A concise and fairly accurate account of the LBJ White House, but the focus on politics is so sharp that little of Johnson's personality is filtered out. Still, this is a good source of information.

Caro, Robert A. *The Years of Lyndon Johnson— The Path to Power.* New York: Knopf, 1982. Contains great details of Lyndon Johnson's early life but is often repetitive and sometimes works too hard to psychoanalyze LBJ. It is, however, thoroughly researched and contains outstanding material.

Caro, Robert A. *The Years of Lyndon Johnson— Means of Ascent.* New York: Knopf, 1990. It seems that Caro has made Lyndon Johnson his life's work and has determined to make a case against LBJ. This book, as thoroughly researched as the first, draws many more conclusions and may actually exceed the bounds of biographical license. Caro is especially hard on LBJ for his election buying while rarely acknowledging the widespread reports of election buying elsewhere in Johnson's day. He also paints an overzealously unflattering picture of Lady Bird Johnson in this book.

Conkin, Paul K. *Big Daddy from the Pedernales.* Boston: Twayne Publishers, 1986. The title gives the reader an idea of where the author stands on Lyndon Johnson. As do most other Johnson biographers, Conkin has tried to show a pattern of lying and cheating on LBJ's part. It does not add anything to the Caro books.

Dallek, Robert. *Lone Star Rising.* New York: Oxford University Press, 1991. As time passes, LBJ biographies are becoming increasingly balanced and fair to the late president. Dallek's book achieves a better balance than most and is very well researched. It is an excellent source of information about LBJ.

de Toledano, Ralph. *R.F.K. The Man Who Would Be President.* New York: Putnam, 1967. De Toledano was a frequent contributor to the conservative *National Review* magazine, a fact that may have helped him balance his book against the tide of media affection expressed at the time for the Kennedys. It is more reportorial analysis than history, but provides keen insights into the personality of one of LBJ's greatest opponents.

Donovan, Robert J. *A Concise Compendium of the Warren Commission Report on the Assassination of John F. Kennedy.* New York: Popular Library, 1964. The official record edited for popular consumption and missing virtually nothing. Anyone interested in the various conspiracy theories of the 1960s should read this book first.

Dugger, Ronnie. *The Politician, The Life and Times of Lyndon Johnson.* New York: Norton, 1982. The Lyndon Johnson story with lots of contemporary history and personal opinion thrown in. Sometimes this book is hard to read because it lectures about the times and psychological meanings. But there's a lot of good material to dig out of Dugger's book.

Halberstam, David. *The Best and the Brightest.* New York: Random House, 1972. A commentary filled with wit and wisdom. It would take a sophisticated historian to use this book as a source, not because it contains any historical flaws but because it's written more for enlightened entertainment than for any academic purpose. It is well worth reading as background on the Camelot and post-Camelot White House.

Houk, Rose. *Heart's Home.* Austin, Tex.: Southwest Parks and Monuments Association, 1986. This 42-page booklet, available at the LBJ Museum bookstore and many libraries, contains a lot of anecdotal material about Texas Hill Country and the Johnson family. It's easy reading and includes many photos of interest to Johnson buffs and students doing research.

Johnson, Lady Bird. *A White House Diary.* New York: Holt, Rinehart and Winston, 1970. Mrs. Johnson is a very private person, and she did not give up any of her privacy in her diary. You have to squeeze hard to extract any useful information.

Lyndon

Baines

Johnson

Johnson, Lyndon Baines. *The Vantage Point.* New York: Holt, Rinehart and Winston, 1971. Written shortly before LBJ's death, this contains a lot of misinformation as well as history. The main value of the book is as a record of what LBJ wanted to say of himself, but the facts are rarely to be trusted.

Johnson, Rebekah Baines. *A Family Album.* New York: McGraw Hill, 1965. This 146-page book is just what it says it is—a family album. Johnson's mother wrote this while in her eighties largely to pass the time. It is filled with interesting tidbits of LBJ's early years and more photos.

Johnson, Sam Houston. *My Brother Lyndon.* New York: Cowles Book Company, 1970. Like other Johnsons, Sam Houston did not always give the same version of a story that everyone else gave. But if you put all the stories together and cut away the parts that stick out as too odd, you can develop a picture of life among the Johnsons.

Kearns, Doris. *Lyndon Johnson and the American Dream.* New York: Harper & Row, 1976. Doris Kearns is one of the most caring biographers of Lyndon Johnson and is rumored to have been closer to him than a biographer ought to get. She did accept some things Johnson told her as true without doing much checking. Consequently, hers are among the stories that have to be checked against those of other biographers. But she is a capable writer and has made some touching observations of LBJ.

McCarthy, Eugene J. *The Ultimate Tyranny.* New York: Harcourt Brace Jovanovich, 1980. A well-written book whose value lies not in the history it relates so much as in the author's style and out-look. Two-time presidential candidate McCarthy gives us a feeling for the kind of thinking LBJ faced when he made his decision not to run for reelection.

Bibliography

Miller, Merle. *Lyndon, An Oral Biography.* New York: Putnam, 1980. The best history is told by those who lived it, provided it is edited by a clever and careful journalist. The Miller book is just that and is an excellent source of information on LBJ. It is well organized and very interesting to read.

Rostow, W. W. *The Diffusion of Power.* New York: Macmillan, 1972. Contemporary history at its best. It is loaded with data about the economy, but at the same time it provides outstanding anecdotal material about the years between Eisenhower and Nixon, the same years of Lyndon's rapid rise to power and fall from grace. It is very useful.

Schlesinger, Arthur M., Jr. *Robert Kennedy and His Times.* Boston: Houghton Mifflin, 1978. Schlesinger, a first-class historian, was also a Kennedy family adviser. His book is highly recommended to anyone studying the 1960s, the Kennedys, or American political history. There is not much in it for Johnson students, but what little there is has been well researched and written.

Steinberg, Alfred. *Sam Johnson's Boy.* New York: Macmillan, 1968. A lusty journalistic approach to the life of LBJ, with some excellent research. It is very long at 871 pages and the stories are well researched, although perhaps not quite as well as those contained in the Caro books. Still, Steinberg wrote his book during LBJ's presidency, so there was no LBJ Library and no hindsight to work with.

Lyndon

Baines

Johnson

Viorst, Milton. *Fire in the Streets.* New York: Simon and Schuster, 1979. A very good source on the 1960s. It is written with great feeling by a man who was there, covering all the years of Lyndon Johnson's presidency and then some as a newspaper reporter.

Index

Lyndon

Baines

Johnson

Lyndon

Baines

Johnson